A GOOD CAMP

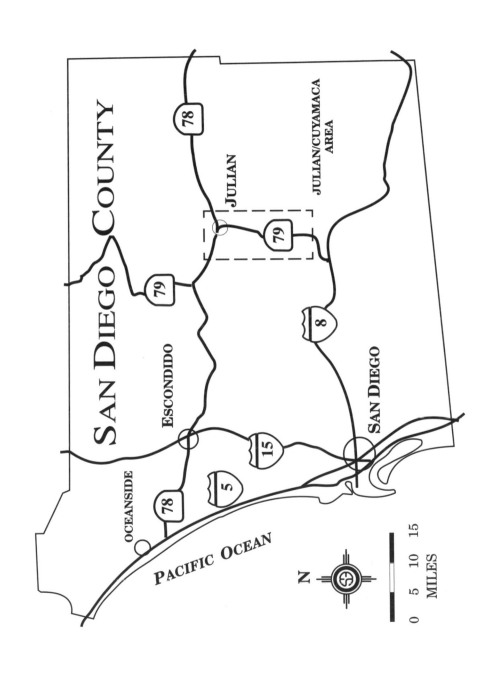

A GOOD CAMP:
GOLD MINES OF JULIAN AND THE CUYAMACAS

LELAND FETZER

Sunbelt Natural History Books
"Adventures in the Natural and Cultural History
of the Californias"

SUNBELT PUBLICATIONS
San Diego, California

A Good Camp
Sunbelt Publications
Copyright © 2002 by the author
All rights reserved. First edition 2002
Book design and composition by W. G. Hample & Associates
Edited by Jennifer Redmond
Cover design by Leah Cooper
Printed in the United States of America

No part of this book may be reproduced in any form without permission
of the Publisher. Please direct comments and inquiries to:

Sunbelt Publication, Inc.
P.O. Box 191126
San Diego, CA 92159-1126
(619) 258-4911 (619) 258-4916 fax
www.sunbeltpub.com

_____

Library of Congress Cataloging—in—Publication Data

Fetzer, Leland.
    A good camp: gold mines of Julian and the Cuyamacas / Leland Fetzer.
        p.cm.— (Adventures in cultural and natural history)
    Includes bibliographical references and index.
      ISBN 0-932653-48-0 (pbk.)
      1. Gold mines and mining—California—San Diego County—
History. 2. San Diego County (Calif.)—Gold discoveries. I. Title.
II. Series.
      F868.S15 F48 2002
        979.4'98—dc21
                                        2002002469

All photos by the author unless otherwise noted.
Cover background photo of "Ranchita Mine" by Leland Fetzer.
Cover photo inset "Pride of the West Mine" courtesy of San Diego
Historical Society, Photograph Collection

The surface rock being rich, it was a good camp for poor men.
(California State Mining Bureau. *Report*, VIII, 1888, p. 513)

CONTENTS

PREFACE

Early in the year 2001, I submitted a book-length manuscript entitled *The Cuyamacas: An Informal History of People in a Southern California Mountain Range, 1772–1972,* to Sunbelt Publications. The editors were pleased with what they saw, one editor writing, "This will become the authoritative guide to the history of the Cuyamacas." It was agreed that the manuscript would see the light of day as a book some time in the future. However—no joy in life is unalloyed—the editors objected to the passages in the manuscript dealing with mines and mining—they were too long, they said. They also observed, and I had to agree with them, that mining didn't seem to fit in well with the rest of the book, which was mostly social history. How could I mix stamp mills with lynchings, roof pendants with apple orchards, overhand stoping with the exploits of Pedro Fages? Cut and trim, the editors said, the fewer passages about mining the better.

It was like telling a new mother that she had a beautiful baby, but the infant would be ever so much more handsome if she would cut off one of his legs and an arm at the elbow. Just when I was contemplating the unpleasant task of reducing the manuscript I received another telephone call from the press. After reconsideration, the editors suggested that I remove the scattered passages of the manuscript that dealt with mines and mining, rearrange and edit them, amplify where necessary, and the result they would publish as a separate book.

After a little hesitation, because I loved my baby just the way he was, warts and all, I agreed to make the changes. With revisions, the new book would have a single unified subject. What's more, I could lift out the scattered sections of the manuscript dealing with mining and bring them all together, so that the resulting product, like all good books, would have a beginning, a middle, and an end. And so it was that *A Good Camp* was born from the manuscript of *The Cuyamacas,* like Eve from Adam's rib.

Another reason I grew to like the idea of creating a new book out of the old was that I recently had discovered an invaluable text just then hot off the press: Michael J. Walawender's *The Peninsular Ranges: A Geological Guide to San Diego's Back Country*. For nearly thirty years Professor Walawender has taught at San Diego State University where he has made a specialty of the geology of the Peninsular Ranges. His book is especially valuable because, unlike older studies, it is based on the theory of plate tectonics, new since the 1960s, that revolutionized the study of geology. I am indebted in many ways to Professor Walawender's text, especially in Chapter 1 of this book.

Rewriting the mining passages in the manuscript also gave me an opportunity to utilize a recent acquisition: copies of the four hundred forgotten letters in the Bancroft Library that Waldo Waterman, Superintendent of the Stonewall Mine, wrote to his father Robert Waterman, owner of the mine from 1886 to 1891. Beyond doubt, this is the best source of information on the history of any Cuyamaca mine, and I was happy to utilize these letters at times in the rewriting of *A Good Camp*.

ACKNOWLEDGMENTS

Many people have contributed to the writing of this book. Thomas Crandall shared with me his incomparable knowledge of the Stonewall Mine's history and provided me with some printed materials that I cite in the book. James Newland, Alexander D. Bevil, and Alexa Luberski of the California State Department of Parks and Recreation were especially helpful with materials also about the Stonewall.

My thanks go to John E. Panter and Dennis Sharp at the San Diego Historical Archives who were always ready to help. The Photograph Collection of the Society provided early mining photographs. Mable Carlson and Edwina Silbernagel at the Julian Pioneer Museum made their files available to me. I would also like to express my thanks to Don Albright and Richard Cerutti of the San Diego Natural History Museum who introduced me to Cuyamaca geology. Special thanks go to Peaches Rudisill at the Banner Store, Bob Atkins of the K.Q. Ranch, Dain Blackburn, owner of the Ready Relief, Redman, and Hubbard Mines and partial owner of the Warlock Mine, and Frank Cozart who shared with me their knowledge of the Banner mines, and to Harlan Nelson, operator of Eagle Mine tours.

Robin Alter-Haas and Steve Scott played a special and very important role in the writing of the book: it was they who steered a slow learner as best they could through the mazes of contemporary computer usage. I can say without question that without them this book would never have been written—at least on a computer.

Finally, I want to thank Richard H. Lawson for his help in improving the book's style and removing from it uncounted blemishes. The book profited greatly from his corrections and suggestions.

Leland Fetzer
San Diego, California

INTRODUCTION

Sometime in the winter of 1870 a former Kentucky slave named Frederick (Fred) Coleman discovered placer gold in the sands of the little creek south and west of Julian that still bears his name. When the word went out about Coleman's discoveries, prospectors flocked to the district. They didn't find much gold in Coleman Creek, just enough to pay them a few dollars a day. The result was something called the Coleman Mining District and a tent town called Emily City. Both the district and the camp remain obscure; nothing much survives about them but their names.

Concluding rightly that the placer gold came from somewhere above the creek, newly arrived prospectors concentrated their searches on nearby hillsides. So it was on February 20, 1870, that Drury Bailey made the first hard rock strike in quartz on a ridge known as Gold Hill just above what came to be the town of Julian, a claim he called the Warrior's Rest. But he and his cousins saw the claim was worthless because it held only a small pocket of ore, and so it was the George Washington Mine, discovered on February 22, 1870, that claims the distinction of becoming the Cuyamacas' first producing gold mine. Even before this date, in anticipation of gold strikes, the prospectors had organized the Julian Mining District with Michael Julian as recorder. Drury Bailey, who had taken up a squatter's claim on 160 acres at the foot of Gold Hill, began to think about organizing a town site.

Within a few months the *Julian Mining Records* recorded more than fifty claims on Gold Hill and elsewhere east of the town. Ten miles to the south Englishman Charles Hensley made a promising strike on a hillock overlooking what is today's Cuyamaca Reservoir. Someone, but probably not Hensley, named it the Stonewall Jackson Mine to honor the Confederate general. For the next twenty years, under a variety of owners, it would yield a full but erratic stream of bullion, some 40% of all the gold found in the Cuyamacas.

In August 1870 an assayer named Louis Redman made another promising strike about five miles east and about 1,500 feet lower than Gold Hill in a steep canyon leading to the desert. When he planted a flag to mark the spot, he began a rush to the new district where prospectors found richer strikes than on Gold Hill. To celebrate Redman's banner, nearby San Felipe Creek was renamed Banner Creek. With the discovery of more gold, miners established the Banner Mining District. A rag-tag town, Banner, arose on a flat near the creek.

In seven brief and hectic years, miners would take about $1,700,000 in gold from the area, more than half of all the wealth that ever came from the Julian-Banner District. These were the boom years, when a miner could pick up gold from the surface or find it in a fifty-foot shaft with a thirty-foot drift on the lode.

But the boom collapsed after 1876, and for nearly fifteen years the Cuyamaca mines were in borrasca, the very opposite of bonanza. However, from 1888 to about 1902 the mines revived, for a number of reasons. New money for mining investment arrived with the transcontinental railroad in San Diego, prospectors discovered the Gold King and Gold Queen Mines (bubbles that burst) and the Ranchita Mine, and the Stonewall Mine's production soared when a new owner with deep pockets bought the mine in 1886.

The twentieth century was not kind to Cuyamaca mining. After the boom of the 1890s, a hundred years of twentieth century gold production was only a small fraction of what thirty years in the nineteenth century had yielded. In 1933, thanks to insignificant mining activity, the books of the combined Julian and Banner Districts were transferred to San Diego. Yes, some mines were revived from time to time, and twice in the century dramatic increases in the price of gold stirred hopes for a revival of the district, but all the plans for developing new and rich Cuyamaca mines died aborning.

But the mines cannot be forgotten. They changed the face of the mountains with excavations and mine buildings, roads, and private inholdings, brought a surge of prosperity to what would have been only a modest ranching and farming district, and attracted a mixed population of emigrants and settlers from other regions who would never had come if the gold had not drawn them to the mountains.

And most important, now that a hundred and thirty years has passed since Fred Coleman panned the first flakes of Julian gold, we can see that the mines created something else: a colorful community unique in southern California, and one heavy with reminders of the past. In expectation of enriching their own lives, modern visitors in unexpected numbers come to savor that town's past, vicariously to live again in a world promising the lure of hidden bonanzas, to understand something about the trials and triumphs of early Cuyamaca gold mining. To increase and to deepen that understanding is the purpose of this book.

Note. All gold production figures in the book are given in nineteenth century dollars. In 1870 the price of gold was less than $20.00 an ounce, while today it's about $260.00 an ounce, or thirteen times higher. However, wages and living costs have also increased enormously in the last 130 years—a Julian miner earned $2.50 a day, while today's hard rock miner earns about $160.00 a day, or sixty-four times more than the Julian miner.

CHAPTER 1
WHERE THE GOLD CAME FROM

.... I have panned nuggets from streams in Colorado and Northern California, and watched as, on two occasions in the Golden Chariot Mine, finely crushed rock washed over a simple table-like device left behind a gleaming trail of the magic powder. Each time, the excitement was unabated by previous experiences. Surely it must have been that way for the early prospectors in San Diego County—Michael J. Walawender.

A traveler heading east from the city of San Diego cannot fail to note that he has entered new country with a different look. Everywhere he will see rounded masses of whitish rock on such prominent heights as Mount Helix, El Cajon Mountain, and to the north, Mount Woodson. He is now crossing the Peninsular Ranges Batholith, an enormous body of rock perhaps sixty miles wide and six hundred miles long. (It bears this name because it dominates the Peninsular Ranges from Riverside County far into Baja California, and it is called a batholith because it is indeed deep rock which is what the word means in the original Greek.) Probably he would not know that this rock underlies all of San Diego County except a ten-mile strip of land along the coast. He also might not know that this batholith gave birth, one way or another, to Cuyamaca gold.

If you asked the traveler what he calls this omnipresent east county rock he would undoubtedly answer that it was granite—a geologist would probably prefer to call it intrusive igneous rock. It is intrusive because it intruded into the older rocks that stood in its way. In a specialized way intrusive also means that it did not reach the surface; if it did, like lava, it would be called extrusive. It is called igneous because it was hot as fire. The melted rock that once was the batholith geologists call magma, meaning dough in Greek. About a hundred million years ago the enormous batholith, then a molten mass, rose from the depths. Today it is a vast island of cold, white crystalline rock stretching from Mt. San Jacinto to the waist of Baja California.

When the traveler turns off Interstate 8 heading for Cuyamaca Rancho State Park he will see everywhere the remains of the great batholith. If he is observant he may note that in some places the rock is light in color, in some places dark, and that it varies in texture as well. In some places it is fine-grained, while in other places it is knobbed and holds striking crystals. Without entering into the intricacies of mineralogy, this is good evidence that the batholith's magma was not uniform but varied in its makeup, something that geologists have long noted.

If the traveler turns off the highway to the site of the Stonewall Mine within Cuyamaca Rancho State Park, he may take a short stroll to the site of the twenty-stamp mill that Governor Robert Waterman had constructed in 1889–1890. Here he will see fragments of a nondescript brownish flaky rock called schist that resembles nothing that he has seen since he left San Diego. Walking around he knoll where the mine once stood, he may notice outcrops of a twisted gray-white-brown quartzite that is also obviously different from the batholith's rock he can see so prominently on Stonewall Peak above the mine. What he has found is two components of the Julian Schist Series, sometimes shortened to Julian Schist, where gold ultimately found its home.

This formation is called a series because it contains not only schist, which is a soft flaky banded rock with abundant mica, but other kinds of rock as well. Sometimes it is very hard quartzite, the rock the traveler saw cropping out of the hillside not far from the mine. Much further to the east, the Julian Schist Series manifests itself as marble. A few miles away from the mine at the head of Green Valley, the Julian Schist Series contains abundant talc, a soft stone that can be easily carved—the reason for its occurrence at this location is not clear at all. This is steatite or soapstone, and Indians mined it here for untold centuries; soapstone arrow straighteners, pipes, and bowls from the Julian Schist Series are found all over southern California.

More than two hundred fifty million years ago on the site where the Julian Schist Series originated, stretched a low-lying seashore with a mountain range to the east. (This was long before the appearance of the batholith; the Julian Schist Series is much older than any of the batholith's rocks.) Sometimes coastal streams carried mud into the sea that accumulated in layered deposits of what became siltstone or mudstone. At times the streams brought sand that eventually hardened as sandstone. When the water was calm, calcium compounds that it contained precipitated to become limestone. These were sedimentary rocks that flowing water created as it deposited its burden somewhere along this mild coast.

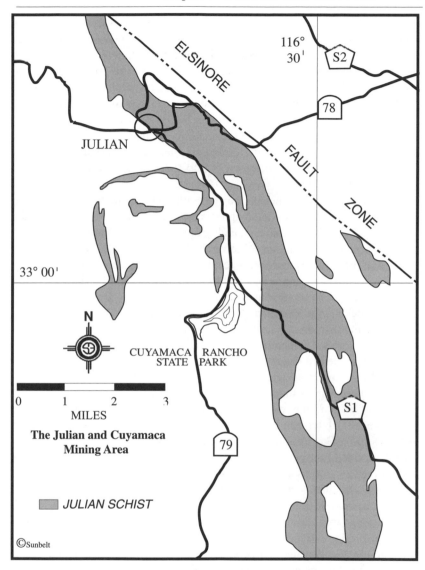

Figure l. This map shows the Julian Schist exposed on the surface of the ground in the Cuyamacas. The gray Julian Schist roof pendant runs from northwest of Julian southeast to Interstate 8. Enclosing it on all sides are the younger igneous rocks of the Peninsular Ranges Batholith. Because it rarely appears on the surface, the map maker chose not to show the Julian Schist at the site of the Stonewall Mine. Compare to similar map on inside back cover. (Modified from Plate I in Weber 1963. CDMG County Report 3.)

With the passage of many millions of years, thick layers of other rock accumulated above these sedimentary rocks. Now, imagine the enormous bulge of underlying hot intrusive igneous rock, the batholith, cooking this package of sedimentary rocks. Imagine titanic crustal movements lifting them from sea level to today's location three to four thousand feet above the sea. Imagine faults crunching the sedimentary layers so that today geologists cannot decide what is up and what is down in the Julian Schist Series. Pressure, heat, and faulting transformed what had been siltstone, sandstone, or limestone into metamorphic rocks, schist, quartzite, and marble. These overwhelming forces transformed ancient sedimentary rocks into today's metamorphic rock, into the Julian Schist Series.

If the traveler knew where to look he could find the Julian Schist Series in other places in the Cuyamacas. It appears as conspicuous road cuts along the Sunrise Highway. It's common enough around Julian and Banner. In fact, the map on page 10 of Professor Walawender's book, *The Peninsular Ranges,* shows that the Julian Schist Series occurs as an archipelago of at least twenty deeply rooted islands, some of them miles long, that rest on the Peninsular Ranges Batholith in many places in San Diego County. Geologists refer to these fragments of older metamorphic rock located on younger batholiths as roof pendants or roof rocks, apt expressions, since they do form a kind of tattered and grossly inadequate roof on batholiths. All over the world these pendants have been a major source of precious metals, and this is true of the Cuyamaca Mountains as well.

Cuyamaca Miners found their gold mostly in a long curving Julian Schist Series roof pendant that curves like a boomerang from just north of Julian south almost to Interstate 8. Most of the boomerang lies along a long ridge that rises above Banner and turns up Chariot Canyon. They also found gold in a small isolated roof pendant at the Stonewall Mine and in other roof rocks ringing the Cuyamacas at Descanso and Boulder Creek and elsewhere.

The classic theory that explains the presence of gold in quartz veins asserts that ultimately the source of the gold was the magma itself. From above, ground water migrated downward through volcanic rocks overlying the batholith. As this surface water became heated through contact with the fresh volcanic cover, it leached out certain metallic elements such as gold. Heat sent the ground water, now very hot, upward, carrying minerals with it. Gravity returned the mineral-laden water to acquire yet more minerals, establishing a pool of circulating water that became richer and richer. Then, much later, over a very long period of time all of the rocks higher above eroded away, leaving the fragmentary roof pendants, their quartz veins, and their gold poised above the cold rock of the batholith.

To complicate the situation, along the most productive mineral belt south of Banner, a bundle of very ancient parallel faults within the Chariot Canyon Fault Zone cracked and sheared the Julian Schist Series. At times movement along the schist actually curled the strata into great distinctive rolls. These faults also served as long narrow avenues along which gold-bearing waters rose towards the surface. As a result of this fault activity, miners had great problems both in locating these discontinuous veins and then following them to extract the ore.

Another great fault, the Elsinore Fault, conspicuously runs up Banner Canyon and past Julian. It is more recent—only a mere two or three million years old—and seems to have had little effect on the deposition or shaping of the Julian gold veins.

Professor Walawender, however, believes it is necessary to modify the classic theory to understand the genesis of Cuyamaca gold. Because the layers of rock were so thick above the Peninsular Ranges Batholith, he theorizes that it was impossible for ground water to approach the magma to concentrate and lift the gold closer to the surface of the earth. Rather, he contends that the gold did not rise from the batholith but originated *within* the Julian Schist Series itself as placers that streams deposited below the eastern range of mountains in the shallow sea where the sedimentary predecessors of the Julian Schist accumulated. These mountain streams, he is convinced, introduced the gold mixed with the sand that eventually became the quartzites, usually mixed with schists, of the Julian Schist Series. The immense heat from the batholith only freed water that was locked chemically within the schist. The water collected and concentrated the placer gold. Then, these superheated, gold-bearing waters rose, especially in the Chariot Canyon Fault Zone, cooling within the roof pendants and leaving quartz veins with the gold. According to Walawender, the batholith contributed only the heat to produce the superheated water that concentrated the gold within the roof pendant, but it did not contribute the gold. That, he contends, came from the Julian Schist Series itself.

But whatever theory is correct, whether the gold originated from the younger batholith or came from ancient sediments that eventually became metamorphic schist and quartzite, the end result is the same: Cuyamaca gold is in quartz veins within Julian Schist Series roof pendants resting on the Peninsular Ranges Batholith.

Only one question remains unanswered: what were the origins of the batholith that played such an essential role in the depositing of Julian's gold? Geologists explain that a hundred million years ago two gigantic tectonic plates once met uneasily along the west coast of North America. (The San Andreas Fault did not yet exist.) The oceanic plate, not today's Pacific Plate but a

Figure 2. What's left of the Watermans' twenty-stamp mill at the Stonewall Mine. Visitors inspect the massive mill foundation, required because of the tremendous vibrations that six tons of stamps made when they smashed into the batteries. One of the visitors holds the end of the four-inch line that brought water from the brick reservoir to the mill. Ore flowed directly from the nearby mine to this mill on a conveyor belt.

predecessor, the Farallon Plate, was plunging eastward under the North American Plate, a process that geologists call subduction. As the Farallon Plate slid deep into the earth's crust, it heated, and its rock, now magma, rose upward like gigantic bubbles to make the Peninsular Ranges Batholith.

Today, what remains to be seen of that molten mass are hills, mountains, and mesas displaying a sea of white crystalline rocks that most people call granite. Resting on the sea of stone are deeply rooted islands of a different rock, the Julian Schist Series. And within the series, here and there, are quartz veins with gold.

CHAPTER 2
GOLD IN THE CUYAMACAS!

Of course, the arrival of so large a quantity of rich gold bearing quartz created intense excitement in town. A stampede immediately ensued, and the road has now for several days been lined with teams of every description, and men mounted and on foot, en route to the mines.—The San Diego Union, March 10,1870.

Not long after the United States conquest of California, prospectors turned to the Cuyamacas in search of gold. They had observed that these mountains displayed promising Sierra-like granite that might hold a bonanza for the lucky finder. According to Dr. George McKinstry, a physician who knew the back-country well, prospectors were scouring the Cuyamacas for gold as early as 1860. His diary for that year contains clipped references to "Quartz hunting" (September 23, 1860), "[Robert] Groom prospecting" (September 27), and "Bob and Jack went prospecting" (December 10), but these efforts led to nothing. Doubtless other prospectors as well sought gold in the Cuyamacas but no one recorded their efforts.

In the year 1861, someone found at least a show of Cuyamaca gold. On August 20 that year the County Recorder Office's records indicate that six men organized the Cuyamaca Mining Co., their mine located on the eastern side of Big Guatay Valley somewhere near Samataguma Creek between to-day's Guatay and Descanso. They included five men from the Cuyamacas, James Ruler Lassitor, John McNulty, Moses Manasse, H. C. Adams, José Mogart, and one San Diego businessman, Joshua Sloane. They located the mine on property belonging to one of them, Moses Manasse, who had established a store in San Diego in 1853 but also owned Cuyamaca ranchland. However, no evidence exists that the Cuyamaca Mining Co. ever extracted significant amounts of gold from its mine, and so it faded away, remaining only a footnote, a beginning, in the mountains' mining history.

Twenty miles to the north, in pleasant hill country poised on the saddle at the foot of the Volcans, lay the district that would become the center of mining in the Cuyamacas. Within easy view of many travelers who took the short cut from Santa Ysabel to San Felipe, it was only a few miles away from where Dr. McKinstry's prospector friends had searched in vain for gold in 1860. In the summer of 1869 it was still ranch country with a scattering of homesteads, but soon it would become the Julian Mining District.

In November 1869, four young bachelor cousins arrived in the district. They were Confederate veterans from Georgia, the Bailey brothers, Drury (often called Drue) and James, and the Julian brothers, Michael and Alfred Webb Julian. Another Bailey brother, Frank, would join them shortly. One or another of the cousins, but especially Drury Bailey, would play prominent roles in the Julian mines well into the twentieth century.

Fleeing unstable social conditions and economic disaster after the Civil War, in 1867 the Baileys and Julians had headed west to the Rocky Mountains to find their fortunes. Here, no doubt, they gained valuable mining experience. Separated from the others, Drury, the most enterprising of the lot, worked for a time in Montana mines, but they all met again in the boom town of White Pine, Nevada. After visiting Arizona, together they came to San Bernardino where they prospected unsuccessfully along local creeks. The date was October 1869.

Somehow Frank Bailey had become separated from the party, but the remaining four cousins found themselves in northern San Diego County in the vicinity of Temecula, still searching for gold. Running low on supplies, the men sent James Bailey on a sortie into San Diego for necessaries and to obtain information about the district. On the road he met a Cuyamaca storekeeper, John Wesley Harrall (there are variant spellings), who convinced him that land at the foot of the Volcans possessed everything a man might want: mild climate, rich soil, wild hogs for the butchering, and streams waiting to be prospected. James Bailey returned to Temecula, and a short time later the cousins went to the mountains.

The cousins took a liking to the northern Cuyamacas. This was especially true of Drury Bailey, who claimed squatter's rights on 160 acres and built a cabin above what came to be called Coleman Creek. After the gold strikes this would become the site of Julian City. No doubt the Baileys and the Julians prospected along the streams in the area.

However, in spite of the important role the Baileys and the Julians played in Cuyamaca mining, they were not the first to discover Cuyamaca gold—that distinction belongs to an almost forgotten man, Frederick (Fred) Coleman, sometimes referred to as A. H. Coleman.

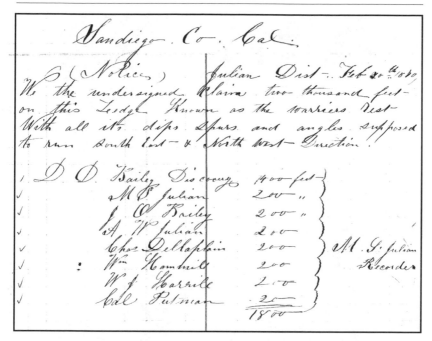

Figure 3. The first entry in the Julian Mining Records, *the claim for the Warrior's Rest Mine with its eight owners, Drury Bailey Discoverer. The date is February 20, 1870. The claims were measured from a marker located at the strike, not by any surveying records, a custom that could lead to disputes. Because nothing of substance was found on the claim, the claimants soon abandoned the Warrior's Rest, and the honor of being Julian's first hard rock mine would go to the George Washington Mine, discovered two days later. (Courtesy of San Diego Historical Society Photograph Collection.)*

Frederick (Fred) Coleman, the man who discovered gold in Coleman Creek (a stream named for him that flows south of Julian into the San Diego River), at the time of the discovery was a 41-year-old African-American native of Kentucky. As early as 1863 he appeared on the County Assessment List as a possessor of $245.00 in livestock. Apparently residing in the district until his death at about the turn of the century, his name appears in numerous early documents; in the 1880 census he and his Indian wife Maria are listed along with the names of their eleven children. Coleman may have learned mining in northern California, but that is conjecture. As a black native of Kentucky he was very probably a former slave.

Evidence that Coleman discovered gold near Julian comes from articles that appeared in *The San Diego Union* in February and March 1870 when the gold strikes were still news. On February 17, 1870, on the eve of the first hard

Figure 4. This securely locked rabbit hole is all that remains of the George Washington Mine tunnel. Over the years, loose earth and rock at tunnel collars often collapse, blocking access to the mines. Chaparral and trees sprout in the loose earth, further concealing mine entrances. Also, for safety's sake in the twentieth century miners often bulldozed mine entrances. But still, this is where Julian mining began.

rock gold strikes, this is what *The San Diego Union* had to say about rumors of gold in Coleman Creek.

MINING MATTERS. We do not hear of any rich strikes as yet. A district has been organized about 60 miles from this city near the San Isabel Ranch, called the Coleman district. There are some seventy-five prospectors on the ground, some of whom are putting in sluices to give the placers a fair test. An old placer miner informs us that these are surface diggings, and there are no indications of any considerable deposits. Another person, long a resident of that section, says that the existence of gold placers there has been known for many years, but they have attracted little attention, because past prospecting proved that none of them would pay over $1.50 or $2 per day.

On March 10, 1870, the newspaper was explicit about Coleman's part in the discovery, writing that "About six weeks ago, placers were discovered in the neighborhood of the Cuyamaca mountains some sixty miles from the city, by Mr. Coleman, who has a ranch in that section."

Seventy years later, Dan Forrest Taylor in his *Julian Gold* (1939, p. 2) asserted that Coleman not only found the first gold, he was working in the district long before anyone else: "...the discovery of gold in the Julian district was first recorded in January 1869, by a man whose name was written 'A. H. Coleman.'" Later Taylor concludes that "A. H. Coleman" was in fact Frederick Coleman. Unfortunately, Taylor does not supply the source of his information.

I can find only one reference to "A. H. Coleman" in the early records. The entry for the Washington Mine Claim in Book A, p. 6, of the *Julian Mining Records* says "Filed by A. H. Colman [sic] Camp Recorder" and then again "A. H. Coleman, Camp Recorder." It seems very improbable that there was a second Coleman present, and so I, along with Taylor, presume that "A. H. Coleman" was in fact Frederick Coleman. Why this form of his name was used and what was Coleman's role as Camp Recorder is not clear. Was the title, along with naming the creek and the mining district for him, meant to honor the man who first found gold in the district? Ironically, Camp Recorder Frederick Coleman, according to the 1880 U.S. census, like nearly all former slaves, could not read or write.

The seventy-five prospectors that the newspaper mentions in its first article, besides organizing the Coleman Mining District, all of whose records have been lost, set up a tent town that they called Emily City on the banks of the creek. Unfortunately, no one left a description of the camp and we do not even know who Emily was.

Probably some of the men who joined Coleman in panning the Coleman District were newly arrived local settlers, including the family of the storekeeper John Wesley Harrall with ten children. It was Harrall who enticed the Baileys and the Julians to visit the Cuyamacas. The Webb family had taken up land closer to the Volcans. That winter of 1869–1870 more setters arrived in the Cuyamacas, some of them Southerners headed for Oregon who paused in

Figure 5. In 1969, to commemorate the centenary of Cuyamaca mining, the Julian Historical Society, after purchasing the George Washington Mine, erected this open air museum that houses a collection of mining equipment. The opening to the mine is only a few hundred feet up the hill, while below the museum is a modern recreation of an arrastra, or grinding circle, a simple homemade device for reducing ore to powder.

the mountains for the winter, perhaps to stay. The Skidmore family established a camp in the meadows near the Laguna que se seca, The Lake that Dries Up, Dry Lake, the site of today's Cuyamaca Reservoir, close to what turned out to be the richest gold strike in the Cuyamacas, the Stonewall Mine.

As the newspaper article stated, the placer miners on Coleman Creek found little that was worthwhile. Momentous discoveries would come only when prospectors turned to the second stage in gold prospecting, in the same sequence of events that has transpired in gold-bearing districts around the world. Concluding rightly that gold in the creek had washed down from primary quartz veins in the hillsides above the stream, prospectors began to search for gold in hard rock along the ridge above Drury Bailey's cabin that came to be known as Gold Hill.

Even before any strikes, on February 15, the prospectors organized the Julian Mining District to regulate mine ownership, writing down five articles that a visitor can still read today in the *Julian Mining Records* in the San

Diego Historical Society's Archives: 1) The District was a rectangle of land five miles by four miles "beginning one thousand yards West of Harralls' Store." 2) A Recorder would record all claims. 3) "Locators" were restricted to 200 feet each along a quartz ledge. The discoverer could take two claims. 4) A claim must be registered in fifteen days or be forfeit. 5) A miners' arbitration board would resolve conflicts. Those assembled elected Mike Julian as Julian Mining District Recorder.

On February 20, 1870, Drury Bailey made the district's first quartz gold discovery, "The Warrior's Rest" (Mike Julian spelled it "Warriers Rest".) Drury Bailey duly recorded himself as claimant and discoverer of the Warrior's Rest, as well as the names of his brother James, the two Julians, and four other reliable friends. However, no one moved to develop the Warrior's Rest because they all agreed the claim held only a trace of gold. The honor of discovering the first *producing* mine in Julian goes to a consortium of three prospectors: Henry C. Bickers, a Virginian who had worked in mining districts in Idaho and California, J. T. Gower, a surveyor, and Dr. J. Bruen Wells, a minister. Since they made the strike on Washington's Birthday, February 22, they named that first notable Julian mine the George Washington Mine, registering it on February 26. The mine was located only a few hundred yards above the town site; eventually Julian's Washington Street would lead directly to it.

The three owners shipped some high-grade ore to an assay firm in San Francisco. On March 7 the San Francisco *Daily Alta California* published the first article about the strike. Three days later, March 10, a few days after some high-grade Julian ore was brought for display in the city, *The San Diego Union* had this to say.

> Of course, the arrival of large a quantity of rich gold bearing quartz created intense excitement in town. A stampede immediately ensued, and the road has now for several days been lined with teams of every description, and men mounted and on foot, en route to the mines. From persons who returned yesterday we learn that there are now on the ground not less than six hundred persons, and the number is daily increasing. As to the placers of the same section, there are now altogether about twenty-five men at work with rockers, who are averaging $3 per day to the hand. The rest of the people are scattered over the country prospecting.

It was beginning, all the confusion, privation, exultation, rumors, sleeplessness, greed, discomfort, dreams of fabulous wealth, chicanery, wild claims, back-breaking labor, outrageous speculation, and devastating disappointments that characterized a mining boom town. In the spirit of the times, a correspondent for the *Union* in his first report from the mines on March 17 wrote,

Figure 6. An unnamed mine. Judging from the men's clothes, the photographer took this picture early in the twentieth century, but it illustrates the start of a mine that could have any date after February 1870. The tools are picks and shovels, and the miners remove rock in a wheelbarrow. To make rolling it easier, they have poured a concrete track just wide enough for its single wheel. If they hit pay dirt, they will lay tracks, and the owner will purchase mine cars. The photo is labeled "Poor man's mining." (Courtesy of San Diego Historical Society Photograph Collection.)

Imagine 800 men turned out loose in the mountains, with as little sense and as much "friskiness" as so many horses. The people here are positively wild. Such a thing as a sober thought is unknown. The rumor comes that Tom, Dick or Harry has "struck it" and forthwith the whole camp rushes pell-mell for the new "diggings." People don't sleep here at all (or if they do they are more lucky than I). All night long the ferocious prospectors make the hills resound with their stories of the days adventures. Talk of Babel!

Prospectors busied themselves establishing fresh claims. They registered the Van Wert, the Hammell, and the Ida Mines. Next came the Hayden Mine, the Good Hope, the Owens, and many others. In five weeks miners registered forty claims, in the opinion of a *San Diego Union* reporter who visited the camp

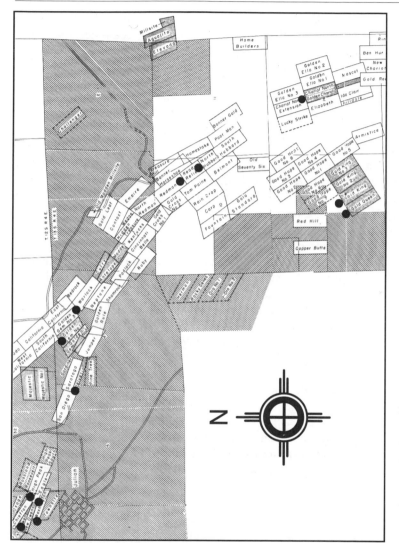

Figure 7. Julian mining claims, a detail from a larger map in Weber's Geology and Mineral Resources*.... Note how the claims follow the outcropping of the Julian Schist Series, as can be seen from the geological map on the inside back cover. Often mining claims were combined or renamed so that Weber's map dating from 1963 often differs from earlier maps. The rectangular shape of the claims, following the northwest-southeast veins, was dictated by their limited width, but unlimited length. Mines described in detail in this book are marked on the map. The Stonewall and Ranchita Mines are off this map.*

on March 29. Obviously, the gold occurred in quartz veins embedded in a long curving outcropping of Julian Schist, but this would become clear only much later. In 1870 the only way to find gold was to search for it on the surface of the ground. In these earlier, simpler, times, gold was, indeed, where you found it.

As yet no one knew the true worth of the discoveries. Newspapers such as the *Daily Alta California, The San Diego Union,* and *The San Diego Bulletin* ran wildly contradictory accounts. On March 16 the *Daily Alta California* reported that the Julian ledges appeared to be shallow detached spurs, only the Chinese could make a living from the Coleman placers (the first mention of Chinese miners in the district), and only about $150 had been taken out of the district. However, *The San Diego Bulletin* was wildly enthusiastic, its reporter stating that three hundred claims had been filed, eight or ten of them worth developing. The same reporter, whom we will forgive for his local bias, asserted that Julian was the richest quartz district ever discovered in California, very high praise indeed.

On March 29 a reporter from *The San Diego Union* visited the new mines, leaving a description of what he saw. Beginning his article with a mild witticism "Julian is what may be called a 'rising town,' not only with reference to its altitude, but as to its rapid settlement and building up," he described Gold Hill and its prospects. Here he saw the Washington, Hayden, San Diego, Kelly, Lincoln, High Peak and Washoe Mines, only just beginning.

Although the district was only two months old, out-of-town experts were already arriving. These the same reporter described as "San Francisco gentlemen," such as "the celebrated mining expert, Mr. G. Kustel, who I am told, expresses the opinion that these ledges are rich and that the indications are favorable to permanence."

In the new town of Julian City, preparations had begun to erect a stamp mill, while the Allison sawmill ten miles southeast of town on the slopes of Cuyamaca Peak began providing much needed lumber. Stages were not yet running from San Diego, but the reporter expected they would be soon, covering the forty miles by way of El Cajon "easily in one day," he thought. In the meantime "Prospectors now foot it in by this route in two days." He saw good things happening in the Julian District, but in general the tone of his article was cautious and noncommittal.

CHAPTER 3
THE MINES FLOURISH,
THE MINES ARE THREATENED

...Now give three cheers for Julian, and her hardy sons of toil,
For well I know each manly breast with gratitude doth boil;
For those who helped us in our need, let daughter and let son
Shout with songs of gratitude, that our case is won.

The San Diego Union, December 21, 1873.

No one will ever write a history of all the Julian mines. This is not only because they were numerous—more than fifty mines were registered in the Julian District at the end of August 1870 and more than 120 appear on the Bailey-Chamberlin-Sickler map of 1896—but also because many were only shallow tunnels that granted such insignificant returns to their owners that they do not justify the effort of investigation. However, a glance at Maurice Donnelly's report on the Julian mines that he published in 1934 and F. Harold Weber's report dating from 1963 shows that in fact just eight mines produced more than 90% of all the wealth in the northern Cuyamacas. According to Donnelly, they were the Owens and the Helvetia located close to Julian; the Golden Chariot, Ready Relief, Blue Hill or Gardiner (known today as the Golden Gem), and North Hubbard in the Banner District; and the Stonewall and Ranchita located outside the Julian and Banner Districts. (See the concluding chapter for a summary of Cuyamaca mine production.)

Certainly a book on Cuyamaca mining must describe these mines. In addition, I have included the stories of five more mines because they have unusual historical or contemporary interest: the Washington and Eagle-High Peak mines close to Julian, and Banner's Warlock, Gold King and Gold Queen mines. The Julian mines will be described in this chapter, while the other mines will appear in later chapters.

The George Washington Mine. On page 6, Book A, of *The Julian Mining Records* appears this entry registering the George Washington claim on February 26, 1870:

> Notice is hereby given that the undersigned claim forty four hundred feet on this Lead Known as the George Washington Ledge. We run and claim Eight Hundred feet Easterly and Thirty six hundred feet Westerly with all its dips spurs and angles and one hundred feet on each Side of Said Ledge for Mining purposes and forewarn all persons from trespassing Hereon.

Following this typical entry in the *Julian Mining Records* is a list of eighteen personal names, the long list needed to claim such a large property. Obviously the owners were pressed to come up with enough names because one entry reads "Proff. Durant." At the time Henry Durant was President of the University of California at Berkeley. Such evasions apparently did not violate the District's bylaws. Mike Julian's name as District Recorder appears at the foot of the entry.

Although the Washington Mine was the district's first producing mine it never came up to its owners' high expectations, remaining forever modest in size and production. On the claim miners dug a hundred-foot tunnel into the hillside and a hundred-foot shaft from the bottom of which they cut a three-hundred-foot drift that followed the path of the gold-ridden quartz vein prospectors had found on the surface, or a total of about five hundred feet of workings. Mary C. Morse, the school teacher wife of the merchant Ephraim W. Morse, visiting Julian in September 1870 not long after the mine's discovery left a brief and inaccurate description of the mine. "We afterwards visited the Washington, the first mine discovered. Here are three tunnels running into the hillside each about 150 feet in length, which we examined following a guide with a lighted candle." She added, " It seemed to me a gloomy place to work...."

A number of owners worked the Washington intermittently from 1870 to 1904 and then again in 1931. The total production of the mine Donnelly estimated at only between $25,000 and $50,000.

In 1969 the Julian Historical Society collected some old mining equipment and placed it under shelter at the site of the Washington Mine, erecting nearby a plaque that commemorates the mine's historic contribution to the Julian Mining District. For information about visiting the Washington, see the Addendum.

The Eagle-High Peak Mine. As the name indicates, this was originally two mines. The Eagle Mine was located just east of the Washington Mine overlooking the town site, and the High Peak Mine was east of the Eagle Mine on the far side of Gold Hill looking to the northeast.

Figure 8. The entrance to the Eagle Mine today. The mine collar proudly displays the date 1870, the year the mine was discovered. The ore car is one of the few that have survived in the district. A standard ore car could hold a ton of rock, could be loaded in a half an hour, and the miner could dump it easily in every direction. The Eagle Mine is one of only two mines in southern California offering public tours.

William Moran, discoverer, and six others registered the Eagle Ledge on April 19, 1870, according to the *Julian Mining Records* (Book A, p. 98.) The owners cut a 358-foot crosscut (a tunnel in search of the ore body) into Gold Hill in a northeast direction. Following the lode, they cut three drifts of 143 feet, 37 feet, and 157 feet, stoping (removing) the ore along the drifts, so that there are no large chambers within the mine. In addition, miners excavated a 260-foot crosscut from a separate entrance point.

Altogether, the mine has about six hundred feet of workings, a rather typical figure for the Julian mines. At an unknown time the Eagle tunnel intercepted the High Peak Mine tunnel, combining the two mines into a single set of workings. Very early on, the owners of the Eagle Mine established a five-stamp mill near the mine collar. Although the building that housed it is gone, the original battery with its five stamps survives today.

According to Weber (p. 143), the Eagle Mine was worked early in the 1870s and sporadically from the 1880s until 1939, and the total value of gold produced from the mine was between $25,000 and $50,000, similar to the Washington Mine.

Sebastian Southiermer and five other men registered the High Peak Mine in the *Julian Mining Records,* (Book A, p. 89) on March 15, 1870. The owners drove a 462-foot tunnel northwest along the quartz vein, making crosscuts at several locations to reach the ore. Eventually the mine had as many as eleven levels with a central 400-foot vertical shaft, or stope, complete with a hoist.

In the High Peak Mine occurred the most notable disaster in the history of Cuyamaca mining. On January 8, 1906, William H. Boswell, who was superintendent of the Helvetia Mine and the High Peak Mines, both owned by the Julian Consolidated Mining and Milling Co., was inspecting the High Peak with a miner, Sidney Pettit, when there was a sudden cave-in. Falling rock killed Pettit instantly, while Boswell managed to reach a safe haven, standing upright for eight hours until a rescue party rescued him and removed Pettit's body. Seemingly, Boswell had survived the rock fall, but four days later he died, apparently the victim of internal injuries.

The High Peak Mine operated off and on from 1870 to 1902, and then again from 1928 to 1932. Like the Washington and the Eagle, it is estimated to have produced between $25,000 and $50,000 in gold, according to Donnelly (p. 352).

Today it is possible for visitors on guided tours to walk through the Eagle-High Peak Mine, entering at the Eagle tunnel and emerging at the entrance to the High Peak. See the Addendum for more information about the Eagle-High Peak walking tour.

The Owens Mine. According to the *Julian Mining Records* (Book A, p. 32), on March 11, 1870, James Kelly, J. E. Pember, Barney Owens and Frank Murphy located the Owens Ledge immediately northeast of the George Washington Mine. Eventually, with its $450,000 total production, the Owens Mine became the largest producer on Gold Hill and tied the Helvetia Mine as the fourth richest in the Cuyamacas. Early discoveries encouraged the mine's owners to install a ten-stamp mill at the mine site, a typical strategy at the biggest mines.

In October 1872 a reporter for the *San Diego Daily World* descended into the Owens, accompanied by one of its owners, a Mr. Summers, getting a glimpse of what hard rock mining was all about. His first heart-stopping experience was dropping down a vertical 270-foot shaft with his companion in an open ore bucket—the only way into the mine—followed by a glimpse of miners at work.

> You get into a bucket, putting in one foot and leaving the other out to prevent your catching on the walls and bruising yourself. Another fellow

Figure 9. Five-stamp and one-stamp mills at the Eagle Mine today. The five-stamp mill is one of only two surviving in the district. Striking in the picture are the massive belts, once connecting with the steam engine that drove the mechanism to lift the stamps; they dropped by their own weight. At the peak of the Cuyamaca mining boom, seventy-five stamps pounded here and at nearby mills. (A photo of the other surviving mill at the Ranchita is in a later chapter.)

does the same on the other side of the bucket.... If he is lighter or a heavier weight than you, it is an instant...speculation as to whether the bucket wont tip over and land you kerslosh at the foot of the 270 foot shaft down which you are shooting into the Owens mine.... You are lowered gently for precisely four feet and then the very devil seems to get possession of the man at the wheel.... He drops you like a shot twenty feet without drawing breath.... You are now come with a thump against the wall.... The last seventy-five feet were a deviation from the vertical line...and we were scraped along this oblique incline....

We at once began plunging along corridors which had been hewed out by the miners' tireless pick, and which reminds one of nothing so much as the interior of a Pennsylvania coal pit. There was the same tramway for tunning out the dirt, and the only difference observable was that the coal pit passage ways were a little narrower and that instead of the "black diamond" display you looked upon...solid quartz, ribbed with gold.... When we came to our journey's end, we ran upon a couple of athletic fellows, who with pick and shovel were busy picking and pounding the treasure....

After a mine had been established, it was common practice to assess stockholders to make improvements in the mine. Needless to say, stockholders often resisted the assessments, sometimes ironically called "Irish dividends," insisting that they wished to profit from the mine, not spend their own hard-earned money on its development. Especially they might resist paying assessments if they had reason to believe that the mine was not rich enough to return their investment in the form of dividends. On February 15, 1874, the *Daily World* carried an announcement that six of the Owens Mine's stockholders were delinquent in paying assessments of $9,800 and their stock would be sold at public auction—the results are not known.

The stockholders' refusal to pay the assessments was probably evidence that the mine had already seen its best days. More than most Julian mines the Owens depended on rich surface ores that initially returned extravagant profits. By 1875, five years after its discovery, it appears, the Owens had passed the peak of its production and begun a decline from which it never really recovered.

The leader in the mine's development seems to have been James Kelly, whose name appears on the original claim. About 1873 he began to sell out his holdings in the mine—did he have inside information about the mine's lack of potential?—using the proceeds to buy a tract of land measuring between three and four thousand acres on the front of North Peak that he made into the Anahuac Ranch or the Kelly Ranch. In 1910 Ed Fletcher and his backers bought it from his heirs, the first of many acquisitions that made Fletcher the largest landowner in the Cuyamacas.

The Owens lay idle until 1884 when it was reopened and worked for a few years. In 1886 a banker from San Francisco, H. J. Booth, bought the mine for only $40,000, an indication of the mine's low status, deepening its shafts, installing new hoists, and renovating the mill. But his investment was of no avail, since the California Bureau of Mines *Report* for 1890 said the mine was idle. During the period 1890–1910 promoters worked the mine intermittently, in 1904 producing 13,000 ounces of silver and 104,000 pounds of copper, unusual metals for the Julian District. According to Weber (pp. 131–32) the Owens was idle after 1910.

Figure 10. The Owens Mine was the most productive mine on Gold Hill close to Julian. As can be seen from this handsome photograph, its developers made full use of gravity: the mine was highest, so that ore cars could be rolled downhill to the ten-stamp mill. Once in the mill, ore moved with gravity from rock crushers to the stamps, and then flowed across sloping plates where mercury captured the gold. Tailings went out the door. For scale see the figures on the left. (Courtesy of San Diego Historical Society Photograph Collection.)

The developers of the Owens followed the classic plan to find and extract ore that lay underfoot. They sank a single vertical shaft that ultimately became 350 feet deep. Down the shaft went the miners to work the mine, while up the shaft ascended ore and waste rock. Water collected in the sump at the bottom of the shaft to be pumped to the surface. By 1886 the Owens shaft was 275 feet deep with three levels. At the 100-foot level miners dug horizontal drifts that offered solid footing for stoping out the ore. They traced quartz veins that went 200 feet southeast and 100 feet northwest. At the 200-foot level, drifts went 200 feet one direction and 180 feet in the other, while at the 275-foot level drifts went furthest of all—260 feet southeast and 200 feet northwest. At this date, the Owens had about 1,500 feet of workings, three times more than at the Washington, for example, but much less than at the Stonewall Mine, the largest mine in the Cuyamacas.

Figure 11. The Helvetia Mine was originally located on the hilltop on the left, but in 1887 the owners decided to construct new hoist works with an inclined shaft and a mill in the gully on the right. When the picture was taken in the 1890s ore was still trammed from the old shaft over to a chute on the new hoist works. Barely visible are a boarding house and other buildings. No doubt, two outhouses meant both men and women lived at the mine. (Courtesy of San Diego Historical Society Photograph Collection.)

The Helvetia Mine. This mine, matching the Owens Mine in productivity at $450,000, was located about a mile due east of Julian City, halfway between today's Whispering Pines and Kentwood, on land where private homes now stand. For three decades and more it was one of the most reliable producers in the Julian District. Helvetia is the Latin name for Switzerland—it seems reasonable to surmise that one or more of the mine's founders was from that country, perhaps Sebastian Southiermer, who was associated with the mine from its first days. (Southiermer also discovered the High Peak Mine.)

The Julian Mining Records (Book A, p. 171) lists nine names for the Helvetia claim dated August 4, 1870, led by Southiermer and eight others including Mike Julian. In 1872 Messrs. Wilson and Leuzander purchased the Helvetia, also constructing a stamp mill in Julian City to handle ore from their mine. The Helvetia suffered from lack of water at the mine head, so the owners built their mill some distance from the mine, a response that cost them dearly in transportation expenses. A few years later in 1874, two Julian residents, the improbable Count Dwarakowsky and Solomon Schultz, together with three other local merchants incorporated the Helvetia Mining Co. at the splendid sum of $3,600,000 (36,000 shares offered at $100.00 each).

Whether their public stock offering was successful is not known, but it seems that their action did in fact increase productivity at the mine for some years. On January 16, 1876, when Dwarakowsky reported to the *Union* on the mines currently operating in Julian, he wrote that eighteen miners were at work at the Helvetia Mine, while eight more men were engaged in "cutting wood, burning charcoal, and at other work outside the mine." If his account can be believed, the Helvetia was the most active mine in the region at the time, with Banner's Ready Relief Mine a distant second, with twelve miners at work.

During the early years at the Helvetia Mine, miners sank a 310-foot hilltop shaft with about 300 feet of drifts following the southeast-northwest lode. Here they found a vein two to five feet wide averaging $18.00, about one ounce of gold, per ton. Later, in 1887, from a ravine the miners dug an inclined shaft 225 feet deep with drifts that intercepted the old diggings as well as a new ten-inch vein yielding ore at $20.00 per ton. At this location—in the ravine—the owners built a ten-stamp mill and hoist works under one roof with a boarding house nearby. Visiting photographers loved to snap pictures of these buildings with their eye-catching steeply slanted roofs.

The Helvetia Mine profited from the wave of investments that came into the district in the mid-1890s. In 1896 the Pacific Bank of San Francisco invested money in the mine, but then sold it to Edward W. Sabin of Denver who promoted the mine energetically, making new improvements and employing as many as fifteen men. Efficiency at the mine improved when Sabin introduced the latest innovation in mining technology, pneumatic drills, in 1897 (the Stonewall got its first pneumatic drill in 1887). In 1898 Sabin sold the Helvetia to a fellow Denverite, Egbert B. Moore.

Early in the new century, promoters organized the Julian Consolidated Mining and Milling Co., which purchased the Helvetia, as well as the High Peak and other Julian properties. Investing more than $50,000, they built an impressive state-of-the-art reduction works to treat fifty tons of ore a day, hopefully to recover 98% of the gold from recalcitrant sulfide ore that miners increasingly found at depths of one hundred to three hundred feet. Built on a hillside site, it had a ten-stamp mill, cyanide tanks and some kind of electrical

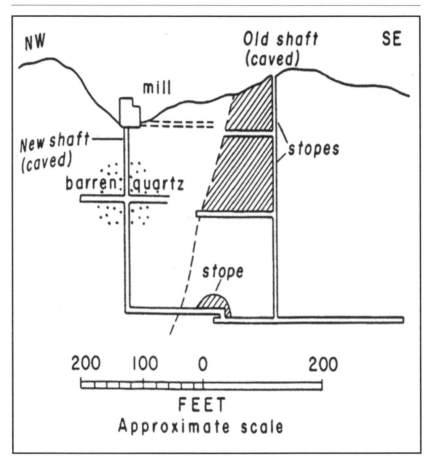

Figure 12. Map of the Helvetia workings. This diagram shows the location of the old and new shafts. It also shows how the miners stoped out most of the ore close to the surface at the original shaft. Eventually they connected the two shafts and pursued the ore at greater depth, but if this sketch is correct they found little deep gold. Total diggings appear to have been about one thousand feet, and by 1963 both of the shafts had caved in. (Weber, Geology and Mineral Resources....)

processing. The owners planned an aerial tramway that was never built to deliver ore from the mines to the reduction works. The plant superintendent was the unfortunate W. Boswell, while the constructing manager and metallurgist, D. G. Jewett, was an expert from out of town. In spite of the hopes of its owners, the plant never went into operation, whether because of technical problems or an inadequate ore supply from the mines is not clear.

Accidents were common in the mines, particularly in the early years of the Helvetia. In 1871 one of the first developers of the mine, George Yost, died in a cave-in, and the same year saw a miner named Miller killed and another named Koerner badly hurt at the Helvetia. In 1906, as noted, a rock fall killed Sidney Pettit and William Boswell at the High Peak. Hard rock mining, then and now, is a dangerous occupation, but particularly this was true in the nineteenth century when safety regulations were not what they are today. In retrospect, underground mining may seem glamorous, but in reality it was dark, dirty, and dangerous work.

In the spring of 1870 the prevailing mood at the Julian mines may have been optimistic, even ebullient, but above the town hovered a dark cloud. In the fall of 1869 four men, Isaac Hartman, Juan Manuel Luco, John Treat, and Robert Allison, had purchased the Cuyamaca Rancho from its original owner, Agustín Olvera. No one yet knew there was gold in the Cuyamacas. In October the new owners had requested the U.S. Surveyor General for California, Sherman Day, in San Francisco, to appoint a surveyor to establish the boundaries of the rancho, a procedure the court required, and an action that attracted little attention at the time. Now the owners predicted that the survey, scheduled for June 1870 with James Pascoe the surveyor, would establish that the newly discovered mines were well within the rancho.

Taken as a group, the four men had considerable experience litigating Mexican land grants. For decades Hartman had served as Olvera's attorney in advancing his claim on the rancho (Hartman received a share of the rancho for his services). Luco had an unsavory reputation thanks to his involvement in fraudulent land claims. Treat also had engaged in some questionable land dealings both in San Francisco and San Diego; perhaps for this reason the Julian miners particularly disliked Treat. (According to a long anonymous poem that *The San Diego Union* printed on December 21, 1873, during the peak of the controversy, the Julian mob once hung Treat in effigy.) Only Robert Allison had no history of questionable involvement in land litigation.

Of the four, only Allison and Treat actually lived on rancho land. Treat was the proprietor of a prosperous dairy farm south of Cuyamaca Valley called the Milk Ranch. Today, a stand of Lombardy poplars south of Cuyamaca Reservoir marks where Treat's farmhouse stood. Robert Allison took up farmland in the Descanso area and timberland on Cuyamaca Peak.

In the litigation to come, the rancho claimants advanced a number of arguments to justify their attempt to "float" (to use a term favored by the Julian miners) Cuyamaca Rancho over the mines. With the claimants' encouragement, John J. Warner, attempting to play the spoiler's role, asserted that he,

Figure 13. The unsuccessful Julian Consolidated Mining and Milling Co. ore process-ing mill. Located on the eastern slope of Gold Hill, it opened for business in January 1906—this photograph was probably taken soon after. It was supposed to treat recal-citrant deeper gold ores with amalgamation, cyanide, and electrical processes, but it does not seem to have been successful. Worth a glance is the young visitor in her Edwardian hat. (Courtesy of San Diego Historical Society Photograph Collection.)

not Olvera, had drawn up the rancho's original diseño, or map. Hence the diseño, the linchpin of the miners' assertion that the rancho lay far south of Julian, was invalid.

One document that the rancho claimants believed was crucial for their cause was a letter dated June 18, 1846, from San Luis Rey, that José Joaquín Ortega wrote, at Governor Pío Pico's request, to the alcalde of San Diego when Olvera was attempting to take possession of the Cuyamaca Rancho. In an English translation, Ortega's brief letter stated: "The tract known by the name of Cuyamaca is in the vicinity of, or bordering on (*colindante con*) Santa Ysa-bel...." The unidentified translator provided two meanings for the Spanish words *colindante con* that are not equivalents. Cuyamaca Rancho was either only in the vicinity of, or it bordered on, Rancho Santa Ysabel; it could not be both. On the interpretation of two words might hang the claimants' case.

A crucial question, however, was whether the letter was an essential legal condition for granting the rancho to Olvera or, as a writer in *The San Diego Union* wrote on June 2, 1870, "...simply a letter of information from one Spanish gentleman to another."

Even before Sherman Day ordered the survey made, the rancho claimants took action. They called a mass meeting with the miners in Julian on May 25 to announce that henceforth mine owners must pay them royalties on ore they extracted from their mines. They also demanded that every mine owner sign a written agreement guaranteeing payment of the royalties.

The meeting must have been tumultuous, with the threat of violence hanging heavy in the air. Obviously, this was a grave threat to the mines, and the community responded to the danger. In the months ahead public-spirited men called meetings where they took up collections. Cakes were auctioned off to extravagant bids, the money going to the cause. And most importantly, the mine owners assessed themselves for the legal fees that would be necessary to fight off the claimants' demands.

From the very first, prominent men in San Diego and the town's largest newspaper, *The San Diego Union,* supported the miners' cause. Perhaps this was out of dislike for the idea of a few men claiming the fruits of the labor of many, but certainly because the rancho owners threatened the stability of the mines, much of whose income flowed to the city for supplies and equipment. Indignantly *The San Diego Union* wrote,

> The grabbers are, forsooth, willing to let the hardworking miners give their time, labor, and means toward the development of mineral wealth, and then not having expended a dollar on their own part, these gentlemen by virtue of a pretended grant will graciously accept a fat percentage of the profits of the miners' toil. A single one of the hardy prospectors who bravely push their way into the wilderness, toiling painfully over the mountains, sleeping on the ground…and periling life continually to open new stores of wealth for the enrichment of the state, is worth to the Commonwealth more than a thousand of the greedy capitalists who leave their lands unimproved and lie in wait for the profit of labor and enterprise of honest men.

On May 28 the first of several meetings was held in San Diego in support of the miners. Participants set up a Defense League with two committees composed of prominent merchants to collect funds and to work with the miners. Early in June Aaron Pauly who had chaired the meeting found a lawyer named George Yale and together the two of them visited Julian.

Just at this time, June 9, San Diego County Surveyor and Deputy U.S. Surveyor designate James Pascoe arrived in the Cuyamacas to run the lines of the Cuyamaca Grant, as Sherman Day had instructed him to do. He began his work in the north at the boundaries of the Santa Ysabel Rancho, and although he did not submit his report until the end of July it was expected that his map would show the mines within Cuyamaca Rancho.

Figure 14. Miners at the Pride of the West Mine, 1900. In fact, the mine was about a mile due west of Julian. The two teams of double-jackers hold their eight-pound hammers at rest as they pose for the photographer. In the foreground is a common item at nineteenth century western mines—a redundant wooden dynamite box. (Courtesy of San Diego Historical Society Photograph Collection.)

To counter his survey, the Defense League hired San Diego civil engineer Charles J. Fox to survey the Cuyamaca Grant also. By the end of July he had completed his work and forwarded his report to San Francisco where Day had already received the results of the official Pascoe survey. Henceforth, the Pascoe and Fox Surveys played decisive roles in the Cuyamaca case. As everyone expected, Pascoe placed the rancho's southern boundary in Green Valley and its northern boundary adjoining Santa Ysabel Rancho in the northwest. It included the Julian mines. Fox's survey followed the rancho boundaries pretty much as they appear on Olvera's original diseño so that the rancho's northern boundary was at North Peak, thereby excluding the Julian mines from Rancho Cuyamaca.

Accompanying Charles J. Fox in his July tour through the mountains was Benjamin J. Hayes, former judge and acknowledged expert on southern

California land titles, also in the pay of the miners. By January 1, 1871, George Yale had left the scene and Hayes was in charge of defending the miners' claims against the rancho owners. Promptly he filed his collection of documents and depositions refuting the rancho claims as *The Julian Mines: Exceptions to the Survey of the Cuyamaca Grant. Before the Surveyor General of California.*

In February 1871, J. R. Hardenbergh succeeded Sherman Day as U.S. Surveyor General for California. In April he closed evidence on the official Pascoe survey. To the delight of the miners, Hardenbergh rejected Pascoe's work, forwarding his decision to Washington for the approval of Willis Drummond, U.S. Land Commissioner. But to the miners' dismay, after a lengthy interval, on August 21, 1872, Drummond rejected Hardenbergh's decision on procedural grounds and returned the entire case to him for reconsideration. Twenty-six months had elapsed since Pascoe and Fox ran their competing surveys and the case had not advanced one jot or tittle.

Reconsidering the grant's boundaries occupied six months from November 1872 to April 1873. In the meantime the claimants repeated their demands for royalties from the mines. In response the miners held another angry meeting in March 1873 where they insisted they would make no compromises, negotiators would be considered enemies, and anyone caught spying for the claimants would be asked to leave the district. Pretty strong stuff.

In June 1873, Hardenbergh announced that he adhered to his former decision favoring the miners' cause and for a second time forwarded his findings to Drummond in Washington. In the summer of 1873 the Defense League hired St. Clair Denver, a lawyer to represent them in Washington. He saw the case through to its conclusion. That event occurred on November 25, 1873, when Willis Drummond issued his statement supporting the miners' position. On November 29 the news reached *The San Diego Union,* which reacted with an article entitled "Good News at Last!"

On January 2, 1874, the *Union* published the full text of Drummond's decision. After summarizing the history of the case, Drummond expressed his conviction that Olvera's diseño was authentic, not drawn by John J. Warner as he claimed, and correctly recorded the rancho's boundaries. About Ortega's letter he had little to say, considering it not relevant to delimiting the grant. On the crucial question of the northern boundary of the rancho, he remarked that "it is evident that Pascoe's official survey of the Cuyamacas includes a large body of land not included in the grant to Agustín Olvera. Pascoe's survey is, therefore, hereby rejected by this office." The claimants appealed the case, but the courts rejected their appeal. Four years after Pascoe arrived in Julian, tranquility returned to the mountains.

To commemorate the coming of peace an anonymous writer in his *San Diego Union* poem, summarizing the major events in the litigation, concluded with these words, accurate, if inelegant:

> ...Now give three cheers for Julian, and her hardy sons of toil,
> For well I know each manly breast with gratitude doth boil;
> For those who helped us in our need, let daughter and let son
> Shout with their songs of gratitude, that our case is won.

In retrospect the long Cuyamaca case seems to have brought only losses. Money earned by the mine owners that should have been invested underground went to pay for the services of such men as George Yale, Benjamin J. Hayes, Charles J. Fox, and St. Clair Denver. The miners' perennial complaint that they lacked funds for investing in their mines gained more credibility. The litigation frightened off investors who did not want to see new owners seize the mines perhaps free of any obligation to the original owners. Certainly the controversy contributed to instability in the mountain region—mining towns are always volatile, thanks to the unpredictability of the ore deposits—and here was yet another reason to write off the town of Julian.

To balance these major losses there was some gain. Because of the litigation, to the mountains came Benjamin J. Hayes who left his invaluable *Julian Mines,* chock-a-block with information about Spaniards in the Cuyamacas, early settlers, and the first months of the mines. No doubt, the history of the Cuyamacas just before and after the American occupation is better documented than any other southern California mountain district, bar none.

CHAPTER 4
BANNER AND BEYOND

The surface rock being rich, it was a good camp for poor men.—
California State Mining Bureau. Report VIII, 1888, p. 513.

What did a Julian miner do when he was hired to work at a mine? He spent most of his six-day-a-week, ten-hour working day engaged in two back-breaking, arm-wrenching tasks: drilling and mucking.

When the Julian mines failed for lack of free-milling gold early in the twentieth century, pneumatic drills were still rare. For most of Julian's history, miners, working alone with a hand-held drill and a four-pound hammer (single jacking), or with a partner, one holding a drill and the other swinging an eight-pound hammer (double jacking), spent the bulk of their time underground hand drilling holes in mostly solid rock, and then mucking up the rock that explosives they placed in the holes had broken free from the mountain.

Simplified, the drilling process went like this. Into the face, preferably above shoulder height so the broken rock would fall down onto the floor of the tunnel, the miners (double jacking was preferred) drilled as many as twenty-two holes as much as thirty inches deep at different angles. Into the holes they inserted dynamite, followed by slow-burning fuses. At the end of the shift, to the call of "Fire in the hole!" they lighted each slow-burning fuse in turn; the explosion would move more rock if the charges went off at different times. If the miners were successful the charge would pull about six cubic yards of rock weighing thirty-two tons and advance the heading about three feet.

The shattered rock miners had to muck, that is, shovel or hand load, into one-ton ore cars. A good mucker was expected to load one ton of rock about every half hour. In a small mine the mucker trammed, or rolled, the full car to its destination. In a large mine a trammer did it for him. In the very largest mines mules trammed the cars; they were unknown in Julian's small mines.

Figure 15. Miners at work in the Ready Relief Mine. This nineteenth century photograph captures the essence of cramped dark underground mining. The two miners are working as double-jack team, one holding a drill while the other swings a sledgehammer. Two candles hung on the rock wall provide the only illumination. What source of light the photographer employed to take this picture is unknown. (Courtesy of San Diego Historical Society Photograph Collection.)

These two tasks, drilling and mucking, took up most of a miner's day, but he had a hundred other chores, as well, such as sharpening his drills, cleaning up tunnels, timbering loose rock (done by specialists in big mines), and many others. A miner's work was not a walk in the park; I have never seen a photograph of an overweight miner.

Who were the miners who dug Julian gold? Fortunately, we have some census records to help answer that question. Early in July 1870, John F. Gould, census taker, counted all the residents of the Julian District he could find. Among them he recorded the names of ninety-two men who said they were gold miners; he didn't have to go beyond Gold Hill to find them, since Redman had not yet made his Banner strike, and no one had yet discovered the Helvetia Ledge, a mile from Julian.

If for our benefit Gould assembled the 1870 miners in one place, we would have seen a crowd of young men—their average age was only 34, with many in their twenties. Nearby hovered only nine wives; the vast majority of the men were bachelors. Of the group, sixty-three, two thirds, had been born in America. Most of them were from the northeastern states and the Midwest. Only fifteen of the miners were from the South. While it is true that the town of Julian was named for a former Confederate first sergeant, and the region's largest mine was named for a Confederate general, few of the early miners were southerners. Of the twenty-nine foreign-born miners, the largest group by far, fifteen men, spoke English with a brogue because they were born in Ireland—even in far-away Julian the Irish potato famine and emigration had left their mark. The remaining twenty-four miners came from eight different countries, no one country predominating.

Later census reports for 1880 and 1900 show some changes (regrettably fire destroyed all the 1890 census reports). The Irish drifted away while young California-born miners took their place. The number of southern-born miners declined. Later reports record a few Mexico-born miners, while the 1880 census records one Chinese miner.

As the quotation from the 1888 report of the California State Mining Bureau that opened this chapter indicates, the gold that miners extracted in the Cuyamacas lay close to the surface. As in countless other Western camps, Cuyamaca gold was rich near the surface of the ground, and grew thinner and more complex with depth. Experts say this is because for millions of years surface water, leaching away lesser rock, left very durable gold. In a sense purifying the gold, ground water also oxidized the ore, dissolving sulfur and other unwanted chemicals. Early self-taught miners liked to believe that the deeper they dug the nearer they approached the source, the mother lode, with its boundless riches. They were wrong. The deeper they dug, after a certain point, the more likely it was that the ore would decline in value.

The depth of the Julian mines reflected the fact that gold was near the surface. The Stonewall, deepest of all, had a shaft something more than six hundred feet deep, while Julian's other major mines reached a depth of only about three hundred feet. Hard rock mines could be very deep; the Empire Mine near Grass Valley descended almost a mile below the surface.

Usually Julian gold was docile "free-milling" metal that a simple mechanical process, crushing, liberated from the quartz matrix. Not pure gold, it was always combined with silver and other metals. The secondary metals lowered the price the miner could get for his gold—usually from a storekeeper he received only twelve or fourteen dollars an ounce for Banner gold, while Julian gold brought about sixteen dollars. Stonewall gold was traditionally higher in value. Truly pure gold, unknown in this district and virtually all others, would bring something over twenty dollars an ounce.

Julian gold was so fine that it was well nigh invisible. Maurice Donnelly in his classic 1934 study of the geology of the Julian District, *Geology and Mineral Deposits of the Julian District,* describes the deposits in these words: "[Cuyamaca gold] occurs in masses from fine hair-like and plate-like particles of submicroscopic size up to coarse grains and nuggets measuring in fractions of inches" (p. 359). Sometimes the miners called it "flour gold." To the point, Lucy Bell King Lane, daughter of George V. King, discoverer of the Golden Chariot Mine, tells a family anecdote about early days at her father's strike, saying that "The richer pieces, carrying gold *as large as grains of wheat* were separated and panned from other ores...." (emphasis mine.)

Very rarely does the word "nugget" appear in Julian mining history. The word, suggesting bulk, heft, mass, weight, blinding presence, and a stunning prize, is lacking from the literature. In search of Julian gold, a prospector patiently picked through the silt puddled on the bottom of his horn spoon or held the chunk of quartz he had pried from the country rock very close to his eyes.

The fact that Julian gold was so fine and therefore inconspicuous may help solve one of the mysteries about the district: why did prospectors take so long to find its gold? Fifteen years before the strikes, in the mid-1850s settlers had taken up homes in Green Valley and near today's Wynola, and by 1870 they were everywhere. Numerous travelers rode the trail between Santa Ysabel and San Felipe over the mountain. But it was not until after Fred Coleman had panned placer gold that prospectors surmised that quartz gold might lie nearby.

As miners burrowed deep below the surface they tended not only to find less gold, it was also no longer free. United in "refractory" or even "rebellious" compounds with nonmetallic elements such as arsenic, or especially sulfur, the gold formed something like crystals that the miners called "sulphurets." Because they would not amalgamate with mercury, handling sulphurets was technically much more difficult, and so mine owners either had to set up their own special equipment or turn their ore over to custom mills, both methods increasing their expenses.

This is how the California State Mining Bureau in its report for 1915 summarized the story of Julian's gold (p. 653):

> At the outset of early operations a substantial zone of secondary enrichment was found, close to the surface, and much rich ore was taken out, some of it having been sold to jewelers for manufacturing purposes. In the course of time these veins were worked down to water level, the free milling ore became exhausted, and with the appearance of sulphide ores, the values became exhausted....

Julian miners had to find a way to free the gold from the quartz enclosing it. The simplest method was to pound it in a hand mortar with a pestle. The product, now like fine sand, they panned in a horn spoon made from a cow's horn flattened into a shallow dish, or a frying pan. This is how Henry C. Bickers, one of the discoverers of the Washington Mine, described his early operations:

I have sold the last [building] lot that I had in San Diego to enable me to open the Washington mine; no other man has furnished a dollar, and I am now superintending the work and pounding out in a small mortar what will buy beefsteaks for myself and half a dozen others. One day last week I had an opportunity of using a two-quart mortar which was kindly loaned me by the Young brothers, and I pounded and panned out $28.

At the next level, at minimal cost, miners could construct a homemade arrastra, an invention dating from early gold mining days in Spain. This was a paved circular basin perhaps ten feet across surrounded by a low wall. From a center post projected a horizontal bar that dragged heavy stones attached to the bar with chains or ropes. A horse or a mule pulled the bar around the post to grind down the ore dumped into the basin. Then the miner panned the powdered ore with water in the traditional way or spread mercury on the floor of the arrastra to combine with the gold.

Neither hand mortars nor arrastras could handle ore in volume. For this a stamp mill was needed. A stamp was a pestle and mortar enlarged a thousand times. In its improved California form a stamp was an iron piston in a frame as tall as a man that lifted and then dropped a few inches about a hundred times a minute into a metal pan, called a battery. Mill workers fed pre-crushed ore into the battery where the stamps pounded it to a fine powder that was combined with water and screened. A steam engine or a water wheel provided the power to raise the stamps. A small mine might have a two-stamp mill. The largest mill ever in the Cuyamacas with twenty stamps worked at the Stonewall Mine. Noisy things, stamp mills shook the earth for a country mile.

After stamps had powdered the ore, the water carried it onto copper plates on which workers had carefully spread mercury. As the crushed ore, called "pulp," flowed over the aprons the gold combined with the mercury to form an amalgam. Operators also dumped mercury into the batteries with the stamps; eventually gold in the batteries would form a ball of amalgam with the mercury. When deemed necessary, operators shut down the mill to cautiously scrape off the amalgam from the aprons and retrieve the balls of amalgam from the batteries (the Stonewall did this about every two weeks). The amalgam they heated in furnaces to drive off the mercury that they recycled for further use, leaving gold that they poured into bars the size of hand soap. To increase the capture of gold, operators sometimes sent the pulp across riffles or even blankets.

Figure 16. Some Julianites pose at an abandoned arrastra on Boulder Creek about 1900. As a sweep, its unknown builders thriftily utilized a local curving alder or syc-amore trunk. Still to be seen is the singletree where the horse, which provided motive power, was harnessed to the sweep. A rock wall enclosed the circle where heavy rocks attached to the sweep ground the ore. (Courtesy of Julian Pioneer Museum.)

The first two stamp mills in Julian were privately owned, but many mines erected their own mills, thereby saving fees and ensuring that no mill owner could steal the miners' gold in his care, something, true or not, that many mine owners devoutly believed. The 1870 census rolls listed twenty-two-year-old William McMechan, property worth $5,500, as "Building a quartz mill," three other men "Working in quartz mill," and Alijah Bichmall, "Amalgamator."

McMechan's two-stamp Pioneer Mill opened just east of Julian on June 9, 1870. In July the Parsons and Cotton ten-stamp mill began its work, while the first mine-owned mill, at the Stonewall Mine, began pounding in September. Late in August in 1870 the Julian mills sent out their first gold shipment. Weighing a little more than 105 ounces, it was loaded onto the steamer *Oriz-aba* in San Diego, destined for the U.S. Mint in San Francisco. At the peak of the boom in 1874 seventy-five stamps were at work in the Julian District.

Presumably in August 1870 the assayer Louis Redman made a discovery that brought prospectors swarming to the district east and over the hill from Julian. According to an oft-repeated tale, he found gold there when seeking wild grapes. Much more plausibly, L. N. Bailey in his 1896 article in the *Julian Banner* described it this way: "In following the slate [i.e., the Julian Schist], and carefully examining all quartz croppings, L. Redman on August 22, 1870, discovered the Redman Mine." The strike was in Chariot Canyon just above where it opened into the San Felipe Valley quite close to today's Highway 78. His discovery initiated a district that produced more wealth than the original strikes on Gold Hill near Julian. It's said that Redman marked his strike with a flag, a banner, giving a new name to the canyon and the stream, a mining district, and a town.

Prospectors worked their way further up what came to be called Chariot Canyon, making promising strikes such as the Ready Relief, the North and South Hubbard, the Golden Chariot, and many more. Prospectors made so many strikes in the district that on November 27, 1870, the miners organized the Banner Mining District. It survived for eleven years, merging with the Julian District in 1881.

Now that many years have passed, it seems obvious that the first Julian strikes were at the northwestern end of the Cuyamaca ore belt because the area was accessible, with nearby roads and houses. After the opening of the productive mines on Gold Hill above Julian, prospectors tended to make discoveries further southeast and away from Julian, beginning with the Helvetia and Banner mines. Prospectors made the last major discovery in the Cuyamacas in 1895 well to the east at the Ranchita Mine on Granite Mountain in Rodriguez Canyon. Gold strikes in the Cuyamacas began in an accessible and populated area and led increasingly to remote eastern locations. Another factor that may have driven prospectors east and away from Julian was the common knowledge that this region lay outside the "float" that the Cuyamaca Rancho claimants sought to assert over the Julian mines.

Mills followed the mines into the Banner District. By the first of the year William McMechan had moved his Pioneer Mill from Julian down into Banner Canyon. Beside his stamp mill, eight or ten arrastras were operating near the new strikes. Finally, at a cramped location in the narrow canyon the town of Banner emerged as a rival to Julian City over the hill. Time would show that it could not contend with the older town, thanks to geography and Julian's role as a market center.

A serious impediment to the growth of the Banner mines and the town of Banner was the lack of a serviceable road connecting Banner with Julian. Although Julian and Banner were only about five miles apart, the former was 1,500 feet higher than the latter. True, a ready-made track, aptly named the Banner Slide, led down the upper reaches of Banner canyon, but it was very rough and steep; teamsters roped logs to the wheels of their wagons on the down grade to prevent runaways. Using Indian labor, by the spring of 1871 a consortium constructed a toll road, well to the south of today's Highway 78, known as the Wilcox Road for its major promoters, L. L. Wilcox and his sons.

Figure 17. Where Banner mining began, a photograph taken in the 1890s. In the right foreground is the Redman Mine while across Chariot Creek is the Ready Relief Mine with its three tunnels that follow the northwest-southeast outcropping of the gold ledge. From Chariot Canyon to the right came the water line that drove the Ready Relief's water wheel. Unfortunately, wildfires, the latest in 1999, destroyed these historic buildings. (Courtesy of San Diego Historical Society Photograph Collection.)

Today, what is left of it, steep, badly eroded, and narrowed by brush, is known as the Old Banner Toll Road.

The most reliable source of information for Cuyamaca's gold production through the years is Maurice Donnelly's report that the State of California published in 1934, *Geology and Mineral Deposits of the Julian District*. On page 352 of the report Donnelly estimated that 1870 gold production was $150,000, a considerable figure, considering that prospectors made the first strikes only late in February and some time was required to start up the mines.

As Donnelly's figures show, the boom years in the district continued at least through 1876, but they were declining by then. In 1871 production rose slightly to $175,000, but in 1872 it soared to $490,000. The year 1873 saw the highest production in the decade, $500,000. In 1874 production dropped to less than half that sum, $190,000, and the years 1875 and 1876 produced only $100,000 each.

The seven years, 1870–1876, produced $1,705,000 in gold in the Julian-Banner Districts. If the cumulative production in these two districts was approximately $3,000,000 (excluding the Stonewall's $2,000,000 outside Julian and Banner) this represented 57% of all the wealth the two districts ever produced, good evidence that the richest ore did indeed lay close to the surface. The mines worked for more than a century after 1876 to produce the remaining 43% of gold from the region.

In the words of one of the historians of the mines, Gale W. Sheldon, Julian "slumbered" from 1877 to about 1888. Census returns for 1880 reflect the decline in mining activity. The 1870 census listed ninety-two gold miners in the district, but ten years later the total had fallen off to only thirty-six men. The California State Mining Bureau's *Report* for 1886 noted the region's declining production, pointing out that its quartz veins were narrow, wood and water were scarce, and the owners had done insufficient exploratory work.

But the Cuyamaca mines were not down for the count. The 1890s saw a major revival, bringing new prosperity to the district. Prospectors made new strikes, and miners found rich veins at some of the old mines as well. The Stonewall, spurred by Governor Waterman's investment in the mine, was in bonanza. The flash-in-the-pan discovery of the Gold King and Gold Queen Mines in 1888 stirred everyone's hopes. In 1895 prospectors discovered the Ranchita and Elevada, far to the east. At the Helvetia and other mines exploratory tunnels revealed fresh quartz veins.

Increasing prosperity in the county stimulated mining activity. In 1885 the transcontinental railroad arrived in San Diego, bringing a real estate boom and enthusiasm for developing the region's resources. Completion of a new million-dollar ore treatment plant in National City raised the mine owners' spirits.

Technical improvements in the industry such as pneumatic drills, diamond drills, and the cyanide process came to the district in these years. Not only did entrepreneurs utilize the cyanide process to treat quartz ores, they also ran old mill tailings through a cyanide solution to reclaim lost gold, for example at the Stonewall and at Banner. A new system for leasing quiescent mines introduced into the district made it possible to mine gold with very little capital investment.

Completion of the San Diego, Cuyamaca, and Eastern Railroad from San Diego to Foster, north of Lakeside, thanks to Robert W. Waterman's support, encouraged mine owners to believe that the coming of the railroad to Julian, with consequent savings in shipping ore and equipment, was imminent. Waterman intended to lay the line through Ramona to Santa Ysabel and Warner's Ranch to join the Southern Pacific at the Colorado. A spur from Santa Ysabel would lead to Julian and Waterman's own Stonewall.

And finally, in the 1890s something began to occur on a large scale that the district's boosters had long sought: out-of-town interests with financial

Figure 18. In spite of its name, the ten-stamp Gold King Mill was not located at the Gold King Mine, but at the center of Banner. Dated October 1, 1895. According to Waldo Waterman, it began operation in 1891, and was a custom mill taking ore from any source, including the early Ranchita. The mill's designers sought to make good use of gravity; ore entered the mill high on the left and moved through the stamps, etc. down the hill. (Courtesy of California Division of Mines and Geology.)

resources were purchasing and upgrading old mines. Pomona, California, and then St. Louis capital bought the Cincinnati Belle and the Gold King and Gold Queen Mines. Oakland capital invested in the Owens Mine. Two out-of-town owners successively bought the Helvetia Mine; the Pacific Bank of San Francisco purchased it and sold it to Denver interests.

As the result of these factors, gold production reached the highest levels in the history of San Diego County, "and most of the gold came from the Julian-Banner mining region," according to Sheldon. Total county production was $560,000 in 1896, $592,000 in 1897, and $673,000 in 1898. The thirty-six miners listed in the 1880 census had grown to sixty-five in the 1900 census, a good indicator of increased activity in the Julian District at the time.

But after 1900 the region began a steep decline in production from which it never recovered. Deeper mining resulted in higher expenses, and the complex sulfide ores that thickened at lower levels were expensive to treat. Prospectors made no important new discoveries. In 1905 production dropped to only $109,000.

Figure 19. The lowest of the three Ready Relief tunnels today. Ore from this tunnel was trammed down to the mill that once stood about a hundred feet from the mine collar behind the photographer's back. Most of the Cuyamaca mine tunnels are obliterated today, but because the Ready Relief tunnel was cut in solid rock it survives.

Cuyamaca gold production was low and erratic during the first thirty years of the new century. The Great Depression lowered labor costs, but the mines in fact produced little gold during that dark age. The price of gold had been $20.67 an ounce from 1834 to 1934, with only the Civil War period seeing a temporary drop in price. It rose to $35.00 in the depression, but this did little to increase Cuyamaca production, according to the statistics. Dealing another blow to the district, a government directive at the onset of World War II closed all gold mines to shunt miners to war work. Even the lifting of the mandatory price of gold in the 1970s, driving its price higher by more than ten times, failed to produce a boom in the district, although it did stimulate optimistic plans for reopening the mines—plans which always fell short of realization.

A statistic that F. Harold Weber supplies in his 1963 report, *Geology and Mineral Resources of San Diego County* (p. 115), illustrates the sharp decline in the Cuyamaca mines in the twentieth century: from the early 1900s until 1963 San Diego County's total gold production was only $150,000, with no doubt little since then. In retrospect, the most significant, if disheartening date in twentieth century mining in the Cuyamacas was July 6, 1933. On that day the Julian Mining District, sixty-three years old, officially closed its books and transferred its records to the County Recorder's Office in San Diego.

CHAPTER 5
BANNER'S BEST MINES

At the Gold King claim a hole has been dug some twelve or fifteen feet in depth, exposing, however, no single vein of any considerable size, but several small stringers of quartz, none of which were more than two or three inches in thickness, but some of which were extremely rich in very coarse gold, some of the hand specimens found here showing gold at rates of probably $40,000 to $50,000 per ton.—W. A. Goodyear, Geologist.

Undoubtedly more gold came from the Banner mines than from the Julian District. Of the eight most productive Cuyamaca mines, two were near Julian, four were "over the hill," near Banner, and two were outside the central districts. More than half of the fifteen Cuyamaca mines that Donnelly listed as producing at least $25,000 in gold were in the Banner District.

The Ready Relief Mine. This mine, belonging to Drury Bailey for most of its life, was the third most productive mine in the Cuyamacas. To its owners it returned $500,000 during its long life. The *Julian Mining Record*s tell us that Bailey found gold on August 30, 1870, listing five additional names on the claim, including Drury's brothers Frank and James and his cousin A. W. Julian. The wording of the claim is unusual: "We the undersigned claim 1,000 feet on these ledges, the Rambling Boy, Local Shaggy, and Ready Relief Ledge.... Said ledges commencing at a stake near the creek [Chariot Creek] and running in a southeasterly direction.... Ledges all supposed to be one ledge. But located to avoid Trubble." (Book A, p. 200).

Sometimes people called the Ready Relief the Bailey Brothers' Mine. Just out of sight from the Banner town site, the mine's surface ore in lower Chariot Canyon was rich, and the miners promptly began grinding it in hand mortars to provide a quick source of cash. They also constructed an arrastra that the mine employed for decades.

This was a few days after Redman discovered the first Banner gold at a location not far from Drury Bailey's Ready Relief. In fact, the two discoverers were close; Bailey grubstaked Redman and eventually married Redman's niece, Annie Laurie Redman, with whom he had twelve children. Eventually, Bailey's interests included four claims in a northwest-southeast row, like dominoes, following the Julian Schist: the North Redman, Redman, Ready Relief and South Hubbard, all known in general as the Ready Relief Mine. If we include the returns from these claims, then the Ready Relief's production would stand much higher among the district's mines.

Supposedly Bailey's fortunes were at a low ebb at the time, but they rose instantly when he struck gold, hence the mine's name. Somehow it seems right and just that Bailey, a pioneer and father of Julian City, should find a reward for his efforts in the reliable Ready Relief. While the vast majority of the district's mines were falling by the wayside, his mine was a steady producer for decades.

In 1874, Bailey sold the Ready Relief to two San Diegans, A. Neyhardt and D. Schuyler, for $45,000, a surprisingly low price considering the riches the mine had produced. Often it happened that an owner sold his mine at a bargain price because he got money in hand, while the purchaser bought the uncertainty of mining gold still hidden underground. At a cost of $50,000 the new owners built a crushing and amalgamation works on the canyon floor. These picturesque and historic buildings survived, although much remodeled and with new milling equipment, until a wildfire in 1999 destroyed them. While excavating for the foundation of these installations, to their advantage the new owners discovered a continuation of the vein descending from the mine tunnels high on the hill above.

In August 1881, when Neyhardt died, Bailey purchased the Ready Relief back from Neyhardt's heirs, beginning a new stage in its history. Bailey operated the mine more or less continually into the twentieth century. Even later, after Bailey's death, the mine operated sporadically.

In the 1888 *Annual Report* of the California State Mining Bureau, the geologist W. A. Goodyear described the Ready Relief Mine in detail, providing a picture of a Julian mine at something like its peak operation. Goodyear based his information on an early inspection of the mine, perhaps in 1871 or 1872, remarking that the owners were just then planning a water-driven wheel to power the mine's stamp mill. Driven by the waters of Chariot Creek, when completed, this homemade twelve-foot wheel powered the mill for many years; it was still intact in 1935. The wheel is a good example of the thriftiness that kept the Ready Relief operating when other mines failed.

The claim measuring one thousand by six hundred feet, the Ready Relief included three tunnels, each about five hundred feet in length, that miners drove into the hillside above the creek, each one higher than the other. Little

Figure 20. The Golden Chariot Mine. Looking north, this early twentieth century photograph shows the numerous facilities at the mine site, but especially the central massive hoist works and the mill below it. Other shafts, etc., are along the hillside. In the distance Chariot Canyon Road climbs over the saddle towards Banner about five miles away. (Courtesy of San Diego Historical Society Photograph Collection.)

water troubled the mine, and the owners had done much timbering to support unstable ground. The lumber for this purpose, "Douglas spruce," they brought from a site two miles away, no doubt towards the head of Banner Grade. Altogether, the Ready Relief had nearly 2,000 feet of workings, making it one of the largest mines in the district.

Goodyear reported that the mine employed twenty men—seventeen in the mine and three in the mill—with wages of $2.50 to $3.00 per day, and "six men on the outside." Workers had built one mile of road and excavated three fourths of a mile of ditch leading to the waterwheel. The ore was quartz containing free gold and pyrites, i.e., sulphurets, treated in the company's ten-stamp mill, which crushed fifteen tons of rock in twenty-four hours, yielding $15.00 per ton. After crushing and amalgamation at the mill the concentrate was run through an arrastra and amalgamated once more, apparently a not uncommon practice in the district. This process yielded an additional $15.00 per ton from the concentrate.

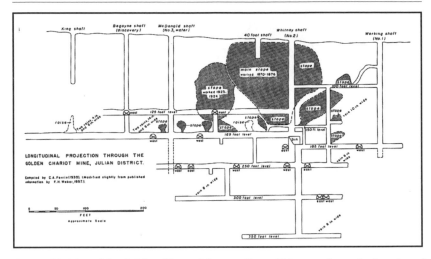

Figure 21. Map of the Golden Chariot Mine workings. This map shows the location of six shafts at the mine, all disposed along a southeast-northwest axis. It also shows the complex system of drifts that miners cut to reach the ore, and the location of the shallow overhand stopes where they found gold—the deepest stope was at the 185-foot level, and the deepest point in the mine was only at the 350-foot level. (Weber, Geology and Mineral Resources....*)*

At the time Goodyear visited the mine, the mill was steam run, the boilers consuming three cords of wood every twenty-four hours. In general, the district's mines burned large amounts of wood to fire the boilers that powered stamp mills, hoists, etc. Timbering must have denuded the hills for miles, helping us understand why visiting experts frequently said lack of sufficient lumber for mine timbering and fuel was a persistent problem for the Julian mines.

Goodyear pointed out that the gold's distribution in the country rock was unexpected. "There is no regular vein to be seen here, the quartz occurring in the form of discontinuous, sometimes curved, sheets, and peculiarly rounded masses (sometimes called kidney or link veins) encased in a conformable crust of slaty matter.... The quartz seems to occur in and among the crushed, rent, and distorted slate along a line of fracture...." (p. 514). The slate is the Julian Schist, occurring along what Michael J. Walawender and others identify as the Chariot Canyon Fault Zone. Movement along the much younger Elsinore Fault often crushed the quartz holding the gold, producing what miners called "sugar quartz," common to the area.

Drury Bailey was a much-respected man in the community that he named for his cousin. The frame house he built for his family in 1876 still stands as a historical landmark in the town. Saying much about the Julian District's relatively modest mineral wealth, the house's simple proportions are a far cry from the mine owners' opulent mansions that still grace western cities such as Salt Lake City, Denver, Spokane, and others. Generous and unassuming, with a fondness for practical jokes, Bailey died in 1921 and is buried in the cemetery above the town.

At the Ready Relief Mine on Memorial Day weekend in 1989 occurred one of the most tragic and disquieting events in recent Cuyamaca mining history. It was tragic because two men died, and disquieting because they lost their lives "defending" property that has not returned a profit for seventy years and probably never will, thanks to the seemingly inexorable decline in the price of gold.

Because some individuals had recently made a placer claim near the mine, the previous owner of the Ready Relief—who apparently thought he was living in 1879 Tombstone and not 1989 southern California—hired an armed guard to "defend" his mine. On the holiday weekend the guard and a friend confronted a large party, also armed, who intended to visit their placer claim. Somehow shots were fired, and the guard and his friend were killed outright. Concluding that the killers had fired in self-defense, the District Attorney refused to file charges against the parties responsible. There the incident ended, leaving a residue of community dissatisfaction and bad feeling that will not dissipate for many years.

The Golden Chariot Mine. George V. King discovered this, the second richest Cuyamaca mine and the richest in the Julian-Banner District, three miles from Banner up what came to be called Chariot Canyon in February 1871, one year after the first strikes on Gold Hill. According to Donnelly's 1934 Report (p. 352), the mine produced $700,000 in gold during its lifetime, most of it when the mine was yet a robust infant.

Because his daughter, Lucy Bell King Lane, left a description of her father's discovery based on family memories, we know something about the mine's first days. She recounts how her father, who came to Banner with the crowd when Redman made his strike, after packing a lunch, passed the miners hard at work at the Ready Relief Mine and continued up the canyon to a site that is close to today's Chariot Canyon Road. Pausing to eat, he glanced at the quartz boulder where he rested and saw the glint of gold. Promptly he marked a two-hundred-foot claim, which he registered with four friends on February 20, 1871, according to the *Julian Mining Records,* (Book A, p. 69).

Every day King and his partners climbed the steep canyon from Banner. Breaking off high-grade ore from the surface of the ground, they pounded it in hand mortars and panned it in horn spoons to give them $4.00 or $5.00 worth of gold a day, enough to buy groceries. Now well fed, they began to sack the best ore that burros transported down a narrow three-mile trail with a thousand-foot drop to the mill at Banner. The first five tons returned them a small fortune, $6,000. (Two years later, King sold out to his partners for $25,000, not the first time that a discoverer sold out for cash rather than face the formidable problems, presumably, that working a mine with partners presented.)

From its earliest days the Golden Chariot was a large producer. In the fall of 1873 the mine was incorporated with 30,000 shares at par value of $100, or $3,000,000, with at least five individuals holding most of the shares. At the end of 1873 the miners noted a taciturn bearded stranger visiting the mine. Given work, he turned out to be an agent for Mark McDonald and W. A. Whitney of San Francisco, who bought the mine for $90,000 in gold coin from its owners. (Although writers have complained that outsiders rarely invested in the mines, this was not true of the two most successful Cuyamaca mines, the Golden Chariot and the Stonewall. Out-of-town men bought them both and got back their purchase price many times over.) The new owners paid $1,790 for the construction of a much-needed road down to Banner that Indians built under the supervision of Joseph Swycaffer. At the mine site the owners erected a ten-stamp mill and steam plant brought from San Francisco.

The Golden Chariot had the most complex workings of all the Cuyamaca mines. To reach the lenticular gold veins characteristic of the Chariot Canyon Fault Zone that lay under the gentle slope where George V. King ate his lunch, miners sank four inclined shafts, as well as two exploratory shafts. These were the 200-foot Working Shaft, the 350-foot Whitney Shaft, the 260-foot McDonald Shaft, and the 165-foot Begoyne Shaft. Drifts at seven levels connected the shafts. King made his original discovery at the site of the Whitney Shaft, and this is where most of the activity took place at the mine. Working from it, miners removed most of the ore from overhand stopes (i.e., overhead) at the 100-foot and 125-foot levels, the shallow levels typical of most Julian mines. According to *The San Diego Union* for April 24, 1874, the Golden Chariot employed more than fifty miners.

The Golden Chariot seems to have escaped the prosperity that came to the Julian District in the 1890s. Weber (p. 124) writes that it was idle from 1877 to 1913 when miners sank the Working Shaft. The mine revived in 1923–24. In the early 1980s a new owner purchased the mine. After clearing the 40-foot exploratory shaft, he renovated and timbered the Working Shaft down to the 185-foot level. All the remaining shafts have caved in. Whether these efforts resulted in significant gold production is not clear. For a description of how to visit the site of the Golden Chariot, see the Addendum, "Visiting the Cuyamaca Mines Today."

Figure 22. A mine superintendent or owner with a visitor at the Golden Chariot Mine. The two men are inspecting an overhead quartz vein that presumably holds gold; some of the quartz has fallen onto the floor. On the right is a typical outcropping of the nearly vertical Julian Schist. Judging from the modern carbide lamps the men are carrying and their clothing, the unknown photographer took this picture in the early twentieth century. (Courtesy of San Diego Historical Society Photograph Collection.)

The North Hubbard Mine (also known as the **Hubbard Mine**). Located in lower Chariot Canyon, it was sandwiched between two Bailey properties, the Ready Relief and the South Hubbard Mines. Supposedly, a man named Mathew Hubbert discovered it not long after Redman's strike in August 1870, but for some reason there is no record of a claim in his name in the *Julian Mining Records*. In this source the earliest record for the North Hubbard Mine is a location claim that George W. Hazzard made on December 30, 1888, in Book E, p. 150. Perhaps Hazzard claimed the North Hubbard because its previous owners failed to do the annual labor the law required to hold a claim. In 1932 the North Hubbard became part of the Ready Relief group of mines.

The North Hubbard Mine consisted of a northeasterly 200-foot tunnel (some sources make this 500 feet deep) leading from the floor of Chariot Canyon. From the end of this tunnel miners cut drifts with stopes where they removed the ore. These extended 500 feet northwest and 200 feet southeast, with a 100-foot winze (a vertical shaft) sunk from the northwest drift. This was a total of about a thousand feet of workings.

Miners revived the North Hubbard in the 1920s and 1930s. In 1921 the California State Mining Bureau (Vol. XVII, p. 377) reported that a five-stamp mill was operating at the mine and six men worked there.

Donnelly states that the North Hubbard produced $200,000 in gold, placing it in a tie with the Golden Gem Mine as the sixth most productive Cuyamaca mine (p. 352).

The Gold King and Gold Queen Mines. These adjoining mines had an unusual history. They were discovered late, their location was unexpected, the surface ore at their sites was unusually rich, and, although it was hoped they would lead the revival of the Julian mines, they failed miserably—according to Donnelly (p. 352) these two mines, which once held such promise, each produced less than $25,000 in gold.

The mines were located at 4,700-foot altitude only about one mile from the Descanso-Julian road, today's Highway 79; the exit to the mines, now on private property, was near Harrison Park Road. Only about 500 feet apart, the Gold King and Gold Queen were about a mile from the Golden Chariot, but a thousand feet higher, and a few miles from the Stonewall Mine. The mines' proximity to the Cuyamacas' two richest mines perhaps contributed to their exaggerated reputations. Claimants registered both mines in the *Julian Mining Records* in April 1888 (Book E, p. 72).

Early visitors were very impressed by the high-grade ore that was discovered on the surface at the mine sites. One of the most enthusiastic reports appeared in the 1888 California State Mining Bureau's *Report*. After describing the Julian mines very briefly, the geologist William Goodyear, writing in a surprisingly unprofessional manner, rendered high praise to the Gold King and Gold Queen after seeing only some rich ore samples and a twelve-foot shaft.

> That this neighborhood [Julian] has not yet been properly explored is shown by the fact that in the early part of this year, in a little valley five miles southeasterly from the town of Julian (at an altitude of four thousand seven hundred feet), seven locations had been made on small, rich veins of auriferous quartz, the croppings carrying free gold to such an extent that it seems almost impossible that for nearly twenty years it should have escaped the eye of the prospector. (p. 513)

Figure 23. A. D. Monroe and C. H. Bacon claimed the Ruby Mine on June 28, 1886, at a location on the steep hillside west of Banner near the Cincinnati Belle and Padlock Mines. In 1892 the same men may have built this five-stamp mill at the site. It also processed ore from the nearby Wilcox Mine. The mill was typical for a small mine— while its initial cost may have been high, it saved hauling bulk ore down the hill to Banner and surrendering it to a mill owner who may or may not have been an honest man. (Courtesy of California Division of Mines and Geology.)

Later in his report he wrote even more extravagantly about the Gold King and Gold Queen:

> At the Gold King claim a hole had been dug some twelve or fifteen feet in depth, exposing, however, no single vein of any considerable size, but several small stringers of quartz, none of which were more than two or three inches in thickness, but some of which were extremely rich in very coarse gold, some of the hand specimens found here showing gold at rates of probably $40,000 to $50,000 per ton. (p. 520)

In 1890 the Gold King Mining Co., headquartered in Pomona, bought the mines for an unspecified sum, along with the Cincinnati Belle Mine near Banner. At the Gold King, miners sank a 134-foot shaft with a 100-foot drift, while the Gold Queen had a 200-foot shaft with a 400-foot drift. Apparently, all the work at the mines was done from 1888 to 1900. In 1896 St. Louis capital bought out the Gold King Mining Co. At first ore had to be hauled to

Banner for processing, but later the owners built a mill at the mine site. Here also were a few houses, a bunkhouse, and a guesthouse for visitors, attracted, no doubt, by the mines' promise, if not their great production record.

Today only a pair of inconspicuous mine dumps on private property mark the location of the Gold King and Gold Queen Mines.

The Golden Gem Group. This mine, or more correctly, the Golden Gem Mines nos. 1, 2, and 3, is located on both sides of the Banner Mine Road at an elevation of about 3,800 feet in the heart of the Banner belt of mines.

This mine illustrates very well the twentieth century tendency to consolidate older mines into a new one, resulting in a single property superimposed on old claims. The Golden Gem Mine occupies what were once the Gardiner, City of Richmond, Blue Hill, Blue Hill no. 2, Canadian, and Big Four Claims. Another consequence of the consolidation is that the property holds a large number of tunnels dug at different times, a number of them caved in. These include the 240-foot Smith Tunnel, the 360-foot Lane Tunnel, the 975-foot Waterman Tunnel, the 375-foot Swayne Tunnel, the Gardiner Tunnel, and others.

It's difficult to learn when the earliest claim was made on this property, since not only did the claims change names, but their owners often acquired them through purchase, not by claiming them. The most important figure at this property was Robert Gardiner (often spelled Gardner) who is mentioned in the *Julian Mining Records* (Book A, p. 66) as holding a Julian claim, the Butler Ledge, as early as January 20, 1872. According to the 1880 census he was a native of Ireland born in 1845. Excavating about four hundred feet in workings, Gardiner successfully operated the Gardiner and adjoining Blue Hill Mines from 1889 to 1900, with the exception of a period of time in 1890 and 1891 when Robert W. Waterman, owner of the Stonewall Mine, bought them from him.

The conditions of the Waterman sale provide an interesting example of how someone could purchase a mine on speculation with very little cash; if the mine succeeded, the buyer could pay the full price with future profits from the mine. Flush from the bonanza at the Stonewall, in the summer of 1890 Waterman bought seven claims including the Blue Hill and Gardiner for $50,000, according to a letter his son Waldo wrote to his father on July 30, 1890. In fact, Waterman paid Gardiner only $2,000, with $1,000 due in six months and $1,000 more in a year. The remaining $46,000 was due in no more than four years, the money to come from 20% of the gross proceeds from the property. Obviously, this meant if the mine did not turn out to be as rich as expected, Waterman would be out only $4,000, perhaps less, if he did not make the expected payments. Waterman died in April 1891, his heirs presumably surrendering any claim on the Gardiner mines.

Figure 24. The mill at the Warlock Mine. The Warlock may be the nearest thing to a ghost mine in the Cuyamacas. Here have survived a mill, a collapsed bunkhouse, a small residence, a locked tunnel, and other reminders of the mining past—but the buildings are not really old, for they date only from the mid-twentieth century. The mill in this photograph may have been used for a flotation process. The view is toward the north looking across Banner Canyon.

On August 13, 1890, Waldo wrote to his father to say he had let a contract to a group of independent miners to dig a tunnel on the property, known today as the Waterman Tunnel. The miner-entrepreneurs took the contract at a price of $9.50 per running foot. The Watermans hoped to intercept at a lower level the rich gold veins that Gardiner had discovered, but apparently they were not successful. By February 8, 1891, Waldo reported that the miners had excavated 450 feet of tunnel. On March 9, 1991, in one of the last letters Waldo mailed before his father's death, after visiting the mine and tunnel, Waldo wrote that he was considering incorporating the Gardiner-Blue Hill Mines for $1,000,000 and selling half the stock. Probably he hoped to restore the Waterman fortunes after the sudden failure of the Stonewall, but nothing appears to have come from this proposal.

In 1936 some of the claims were consolidated to form the Golden Gem Mines nos. 1 and 2, while no. 3 was established in 1957. Donnelly, (p. 352) asserts that the Gardiner Mine produced $200,000 in gold, thereby tying the North Hubbard as the sixth most productive Cuyamaca mine. Robert Gardiner, owner and operator, extracted most of this wealth from the mine in the late nineteenth century.

Figure 25. View from inside an abandoned house at the Warlock Mine. This prospect is from inside the house that probably belonged to the mine foreman or the mine owner. Situated a few hundred feet from the mine under the shelter of a rare oak, the house looks out to the east and the distant Anza-Borrego Desert. Every year that passes, the mine's buildings return closer to the earth, and the chaparral claims more land that once belonged to man.

The Warlock Group. Like the Golden Gem Mine, in the twentieth century owners created the Warlock out of several older claims, including the original Warlock, the Bedrock (formerly called the Chaparral), the Neptune, Shamrock, and part of the East California claim. The Warlock Mine is located at about 3,400-foot elevation just east of the Banner Mine Road. According to the *Julian Mining Records* (Book A, p. 203) George McKean registered the original Warlock claim on October 13, 1870, about one month after Redman's initial Banner discovery. *The San Diego Union* for January 12, 1871, wrote that McKean was running a wooden horse-driven mill at the mine that netted him $100 a day in gold.

The Warlock Mine has the distinction of having the longest tunnel in the Cuyamacas. Heading in a southwest direction, it is 1,660 feet long, and intercepts seven veins on the Kentuck, Cincinnati Belle (or Neptune), and Shamrock claims. Miners made their richest strikes at 1,400 feet on the Shamrock property. Leading from the tunnel, short drifts follow the quartz veins. On the property are also other shafts and tunnels dating from the nineteenth century.

Miners worked at the Warlock in the early 1870s, again in the 1890s and in 1908–1909. In the 1950s, exploratory work was done at the site, but apparently little ore was removed. For a time in the 1960s the mine tunnel was used as an official fallout shelter. According to Donnelly, the Warlock Mine and Shamrock both yielded from $25,000 to $50,000. The Neptune Mine produced less than $25,000 in gold.

A few buildings, mostly collapsed, remain at the mine site. The entrance to the mine is securely locked shut. For a description of a walking tour to the mine see the Addendum, "Seeing the Cuyamaca Mines Today."

Figure 26. What's left of the Stonewall Mine today. The photographer is standing where the Waterman hoist works once towered; before him would have been the three-compartment 600-foot shaft, while to his left would have been the boiler room and hoist machinery, including the Corliss steam engine. Also surviving nearby is a cage that took miners down the shaft and fragments of the three belts that lifted the man cage or brought up ore from the mine. This is what was left after the Dyars had the mine razed in the late 1920s.

CHAPTER 6
THE STONEWALL AND
RANCHITA MINES

On the third level northwest of the shaft a very large body of ore was exposed for a distance of about 130 feet along the drift with varying thickness, which in places was seen to be more than 20 feet and the face of the drift was still in a very heavy body of quartz—Geologist W. A. Goodyear inspecting the Stonewall Mine, October 1889.

The Stonewall Mine. The history of the mine that produced 40%, or $2,000,000, of the Cuyamacas' gold falls into three periods. The first began with the mine's discovery in March 1870, and continued for sixteen unsteady years as the Stonewall Mine's production waxed and waned under owners whose management was not always above reproach. The second period, a brief and glorious chapter in the mine's history, began in the fall of 1886 when Robert W. Waterman purchased the mine and spent much money to develop it, and ended five years later with his death in April 1891 and the mine's closure afterward. Then commenced the unfortunate third period in the mine's history, a story of insignificant production and neglect, marked only by one serious attempt to revive the mine in 1905, until Ralph Dyar, owner of Cuyamaca Rancho, ordered the mine's structures razed in the late 1920s.

Because there is no surviving Cuyamaca equivalent of the *Julian Mining Records* for what came to be known as the Hensley Mining District, the facts of the Stonewall Mine's discovery remain clouded. Investigators have identified at least five individuals who might have first discovered gold at Cuyamaca. Besides the candidate that I and others favor, Charles Hensley, writers have advanced the names of William Skidmore, Fred Coleman, George Hensley, and S. S. Culverwell as discoverers of the mine.

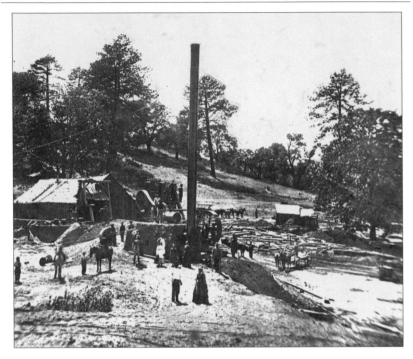

Figure 27. This picture was taken not long after the discovery of the Stonewall Mine. Near the smokestack is a boiler that provided power for the hoist and the ten-stamp mill that stands in the background in the open air (one man perches on it). The ram-shackle building may be a sawmill. In time the mine owners built separate buildings to house the mill and the hoist works. A large party has come to visit the mine—was it the Fourth of July 1872? (Courtesy of San Diego Historical Society Photograph Collection.)

On March 31, 1870, a reporter for *The San Diego Union* wrote down a version of the discovery of the mine based on what one of the parties involved told him. This was very soon after the discovery, when memories were yet fresh, and so the account carries considerable weight.

NEW MINING DISCOVERY. Mr. S. S. Culverwell returned to the city on Monday last from the mines, where he has been on a prospecting tour for several days. He brings intelligence of the discovery of a lead of even greater richness than the Washington, and one which promises to be permanent. The lead lies at the foot of the Cuyamaca mountains, about a mile and a half from the saw-mill, and ten miles from Julian City. The discovery was made by Charles Hensley on Tuesday, March 22d. At a depth of six or eight feet there is a well defined ledge, two feet wide. The ore is of great richness, every piece being thickly studded with gold. The owners of the claim are S. S. Culverwell, Chas. Hensley, [William] Skidmore, and his two sons. The name of the claim is the "Stonewall Jackson." Messrs. Gardner, Knight, Leroy, Culverwell, Capt. J. C. Bogart, and Robt. Polk, purser of the *Oriflamme,* own the first southerly extension, and Messrs. A. P. Frary and Company the first northerly extension. A good working force is now employed in sinking a shaft which it is expected will be fifty feet deep in a few days. Three hundred pounds of the ore will be sent to San Francisco to be worked. Mr. Culverwell expects to put up a quartz mill if the claim develops as well as the indications promise, and is now making arrangements for that purpose.

Ten hours after the discovery there were 500 people on the ground; a miners meeting was held, and a district formed called the Hensley mining district, of which Ed Skidmore [William Skidmore's son] was chosen Recorder. We expect to hear further from this new district in a few days.

Charles Hensley was one of three English-born brothers, Charles, George, and Nicholas, who settled in San Diego. Brother George Hensley wrote that he himself had experience mining in Cornwall, and perhaps this was also true of Charles. George also asserted that Charles discovered the Stonewall Mine.

A persistent tradition credits William Skidmore with the discovery of the mine. Skidmore, whose name appears on the 1870 Cuyamaca census rolls along with those of his sons, George, Edward, and Stephen, had brought his livestock to the mountains for the winter of 1869–1870. While pursuing a mule he found gold on a knoll above Dry Lake, or so the story goes.

According to a variant of this theory, Skidmore in some way was involved in the discovery, at about the same time that Charles Hensley made the strike. For his contribution, the Tennessean Skidmore may have claimed the privilege of naming the mine as a tribute to Confederate General Stonewall Jackson, a name soon abbreviated to the Stonewall Mine because local Union men found the original name unseemly. To honor Hensley the miners gave his name to their mining district.

Knowing that enterprising Americans had recently purchased Cuyamaca Rancho may have discouraged prospectors near the Stonewall strike. In fact, after the dust had settled, on April 15, 1871, the owners of the Stonewall signed a twenty-year lease with the rancho owners, tacitly admitting that their mine was on rancho land. After the U.S. Land Office established firm rancho boundaries all parties conceded that the Stonewall was within the rancho. In order to clarify their title, on December 19, 1874, the mine owners formally purchased the mine and all its equipment from Treat, Allison, Luco, and Hartman for the sum of $6,000, although, of course, those four men never had a thing to do with the mine.

Figure 28. Cyanide operation at the Stonewall Mine, 1898–1899. No book on Cuyamaca mining can omit this stunning picture of the teamsters, employees of Strauss and Shinn Co., who were collecting tailings for cyanide recovery at the Stonewall. The Watermans had built the new 56-foot hoist works, boiler room (two chimneys), twenty-stamp mill (one chimney) with a connecting conveyor belt, etc., in 1889–1890. The wooden building is a sawmill. The photographer faced southwest with his back to the lake when he took this picture. (Courtesy of San Diego Historical Society Photograph Collection.)

According to the newspaper account, twelve men had their names on the original claims. They were an oddly mixed group, including some San Diegans whom the prospect of finding gold had seemingly lured to the Cuyamacas. In addition to farmers, William Skidmore and his two sons, they included a lawyer, Frary; a San Diego businessman, S. S. Culverwell; a ship captain, Bogart; a ship's purser, Polk; an English immigrant, Charles Hensley; and others. Probably several of these men made strikes at about the same time, and so everyone worked out a scheme for shared ownership. However, harmony among the claimants was not to last.

In the course of the next couple of years nearly all of them fell away, leaving only two owners of the Stonewall Mine. The first of these was the lawyer, sometimes called Captain, Almon P. Frary, born in Ohio, who was frequently called on to exercise his legal skills in the next decade in the tangled litigation connected with the Stonewall Mine. Far more legal action was taken over the Stonewall mine than any other in the Cuyamacas; perhaps this was because of its original group ownership, or because it was the richest mine in the district. (Frary is not to be confused with his son, Almon P. Frary, Jr., longtime Julian resident and mine owner who died in 1943.) The second owner was his partner, the housepainter Joseph Farley, aged 24, a native of Illinois with $400 in real estate, according to the 1870 census. His name did not appear in the newspaper article, although he was probably the "and Company" following Frary's name.

The Stonewall ore body resembled a huge rectangular table that was eight hundred feet deep and as much as twenty feet thick, balanced almost vertically on one corner. The table, like all Cuyamaca lodes, was aligned northwest-southeast. Its uppermost corner broke the surface of the ground at a point overlooking today's Cuyamaca Reservoir where Charles Hensley first discovered it. According to Donnelly (p. 337), this tabular lode, the largest ore body in the Cuyamacas, occurred within a small isolated roof pendant that extends from the base of Stonewall Peak to Harrison Park on North Peak.

Near the strike, miners sank a vertical shaft about two hundred feet deep (today it is marked only by a sinkhole); from the shaft they cut horizontal drifts, also northwest-southeast, following the veins. This, of course, was the same plan that miners utilized at other Cuyamaca mines located on flat terrain.

Frary and Farley wasted no time in getting their mine into production, ordering a five-stamp mill that San Diego contractors erected in August 1870. Unfortunately, they did not pay the suppliers for the mill, and so these gentlemen served them a number of mechanic's liens, attaching the mine's equipment and ore. Eventually, with characteristic delay, Frary and Farley paid the bill. They may have found the funds by assessing the mine's stockholders, an action the company took on October 27, 1870.

The mine was rich and producing handsomely. Now several individuals filed suits that questioned the way they had surrendered their shares of ownership in the mine. They found a ready ear, for the courts granted them as a group what came to be known as Lot B, while the heart of the mine was located on Lot A. (In 1886 Waterman bought them all out, as we shall see.)

In June 1871 a reporter from the *San Diego Bulletin* gave a description of the mine as he saw it. Although the mine may have been rich, its owners were spending very little money to develop it.

> The owners had an engine capable of driving ten stamps, although only five were used because of the scarcity of water. The main shaft was 85 feet deep at the bottom of the shaft. One drift ran 185 feet south and another 200 feet north. Twelve-inch timbers were used for lumbering. The shaft was for hoisting and another for passage of workmen. A landing was placed every 16 feet, thus rendering it impossible to have an accident by falling. The hoisting shaft was securely bordered from top to bottom and both drifts had a car and track for the removal of rock and dirt. The hoisting was done by steam power. There was another track

from the top of the shaft to the batteries [of the stamp mill]. A house forty by seventy feet covered the engine and batteries.

As the reporter noted, scarcity of water limited the mine's production. The stamp mill needed water to operate and because of an inadequate supply from the mine it was sometimes reduced to working for only one shift per day. Only after the Watermans took over the mine did they solve the water problem by piping it from a spring high on Cuyamaca Peak to the mine. This was a good example of the way that the Watermans raised the Stonewall's productivity by investing capital in the mine, something earlier owners were not always willing to do.

The mine was producing so well that the owners ordered more equipment. They increased the number of stamps to ten and bought a more powerful steam engine. A reporter for the *Union* on May 31, 1872, said that the mine now employed twenty men, fifteen in the mine and mill, and five woodcutters. Six months later on January 16, 1873, the newspaper reported that the mine had a hundred thousand dollars' worth of equipment. Yet later, the mine purchased a new heavy-duty pump to remove water from the mine. Water in the mine was a concern, particularly during winter rains, and pumps operated around the clock. But unexpectedly, in *The San Diego Union* in October 1874 an article appeared declaring that the mine had been shut down but would shortly resume operations. If the mine was so profitable, why had its owners shut it down?

Although the evidence is scanty, it seems that the mine was in grave difficulty early in 1875. Production had fallen off, and the Stonewall was suffering under a heavy burden of debt that Frary and Farley had incurred using the mine as collateral. Foreclosure loomed.

Because of unpaid debts, on January 8, 1876, the San Diego County Sheriff sold the Stonewall Mine at auction. A prominent San Diego lawyer named Wallace Leach made the highest bid at $3,246, becoming the legal owner of Lot A, seven acres, and everything on it. As the courts had decreed, the adjoining Lot B remained in joint ownership of all the legal claimants to the mine other than Frary and Farley. Leach never attempted to reopen the mine, nor did the claimants to Lot B. In 1883 Leach sold Lot A to Hiram Maybury and James McCoy. In their hands for eight years, from 1876 to 1884, the Stonewall Mine lay idle.

At the end of 1884, Alfred James and Dr. J. E. Fulton paid $7,500 for Lot A from Maybury and McCoy and signed a lease agreement with the owners of Lot B for two years, payments on the lease to be made with revenue from the mine. The owners hired a new mine superintendent, J. S. Buck, who was enthusiastic about the mine's prospects. After preliminary testing, the partners reopened the mine.

Figure 29. William Hosking and Waldo Waterman at the Stonewall Mine. Hosking, a native of Rhode Island, was the trusted mine foreman, while Waldo Waterman was the son of the owner, and mine superintendent. Between them, they took a million dollars from the Stonewall, much of which went to pay off Governor Waterman's creditors. Waldo has apparently been down in the mine, for he wears rubber rain gear. Because the mine was so wet, Waldo protested to his father, "I wouldn't work in the Stonewall for $15 a day!" (Courtesy of San Diego Historical Society Photograph Collection.)

By May 1885 *The San Diego Union* reported that the Stonewall was running "full blast" and speculated that the mine was yielding the magic number of $1,000 per week in gold. By July the paper reported that in a three-month period the mine produced between $18,000 and $20,000 for the new owners. In August, the mine shipped a gold bar to San Diego valued at $2,500, in September a 230 ounce gold bar valued at $4,000, and in October a bar close to 333 ounces in weight, worth more than $5,000.

After a very wet winter that curtailed operations at the mine, production resumed, and the mine shipped a $3,000 bar in March 1886 and a $3,500 gold bar in April. Perhaps it was no accident that the owners provided the press with this information about the spectacular flood of wealth from the mine. With such fireworks they may have hoped to catch the eye of a man with deep pockets to buy the mine they had resurrected from the dead.

As a matter of fact, as early as mid-1885 the newspaper began circulating information that an unidentified buyer was interested in purchasing the Stonewall. More than a year later, on September 30, 1886, *The San Diego Union* told the public that an individual had appeared who had in fact purchased the mine for $150,000. He was Robert W. Waterman, wealthy mine promoter and rancher and Republican candidate for Lieutenant Governor of the state of California.

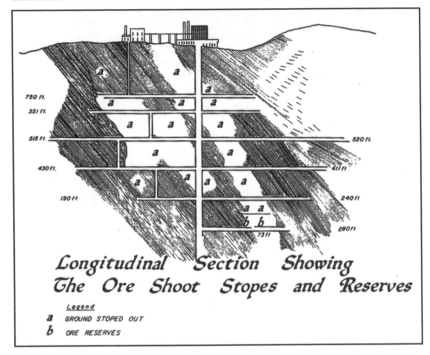

750 ft.
351 ft.
515 ft.
430 ft.
190 ft.
520 ft.
411 ft.
240 ft.
280 ft.
73 ft.

Longitudinal Section Showing The Ore Shoot Stopes and Reserves

Legend
a GROUND STOPED OUT
b ORE RESERVES

Figure 30. Map of the Stonewall Mine. This map shows the old shaft (left) and new Waterman shaft (right) of the Stonewall, which were eventually connected, as well as the extent of the underground drifts. It also shows the stopes where miners found most of the mine's gold at the 300 and 400-foot levels. The deepest level was at six hundred feet. The buildings at the surface are purely imaginary. (Wm. P. Miller, "Descriptive Report on the Stonewall Mine, in McAleer, Stonewall Mine and Cuyamaca City.*)*

Robert Whitney Waterman was an outstanding example of the kind of entrepreneur-practical business man-politician that played a vital role in exploiting the west's mining resources. Typical of such men, Waterman had a powerful urge to acquire and expand his holdings, compelling him to shift money from profitable enterprises to losing projects and to borrow money on a generous scale. In spite of reports to the contrary, when he died his debts exceeded his assets, casting his heirs into near poverty. But there is no doubt that his sound judgment about mining property and the capital he found to invest in it played a crucial role in extracting a fortune from the Stonewall Mine in the late 1880s. Credit, too should be granted to his son, Waldo, trained in mining engineering at the University of California at Berkeley, who devoted four years of his life to making the mine profitable.

Born in 1826, Robert W. Waterman had a trying childhood in New York State before moving with his family to Illinois where he became a storekeeper. After his marriage in 1847 he trekked overland to join his brother in California in 1850 for a try at gold mining. Not particularly successful in the diggings, he returned to Illinois a year or so later. Here he prospered in business and newspaper publishing, acquiring $25,000 in real estate and $10,000 in personal assets, and participating vigorously in the newly founded Republican Party.

In 1873 he returned to California where he took up ranch land in the San Bernardino Mountains in what came to be known as Waterman Canyon. Learning of the silver mines in the Grapevine mining district near today's Barstow, once called Waterman, with his partner John Livingston Porter he combined seventeen claims in a neglected tract to establish the Waterman mines that between 1881 and 1887 produced $1,700,000 in silver. Waterman did no prospecting in unknown ground, but with expert advice identified under-exploited mines, purchased or claimed them by default, invested money, managed them efficiently, and made a million. Something like this he would repeat with the Stonewall.

In August 1886 the Republican Party nominated Waterman for California State Lieutenant Governor. Elected in November, he unexpectedly became governor on September 12, 1887, when Governor Washington Bartlett died. On January 15, 1891, he completed his term as governor, but his party chose not to renominate him for office. Because of his official duties, Waterman spent most of these years in Sacramento and elsewhere, leaving him little time for hands-on involvement in the mine. Writing him many letters, he relied on son Waldo to do his bidding in the day-to-day operation of the mine.

With a flair for exaggeration so typical of mining promoters everywhere, and employing a staccato style typical of a no-nonsense businessman, the newly elected lieutenant governor said this about his acquisition: "The name of the mine is Stonewall. I own it all myself, bought out the partners over a year ago. This mine nets me $500 per day after all expenses are paid—every day. My profit the last 12 months is not short of $200,000. This is the ore on the 230 foot level—next year it should produce $1,000,000. I own 4,500 feet of the lode—the mine will last for years."

Aside from mining, Waterman had many other interests, such as dairying, ranching, and developing a resort, Waterman Hot Springs, in the San Bernardino Mountains. In October 1887 he invested heavily in the San Diego, Cuyamaca, and Eastern Railroad, becoming its sole owner in 1890. Documents hint that the railroad drained his resources, absorbing a goodly share of the money that came out of the ground at the Stonewall.

Figure 31. Inside the engine room at the Stonewall Mine, after February 1890. The three workers are tending a state-of-the-art Corliss steam engine, complete with massive flywheel and Rube Goldberg two-ball governor. The shaft to the left probably connected with the hoist. This engine is typical of the expensive technological improvements Waldo Waterman brought to the Stonewall, unknowingly on the eve of its collapse. (Courtesy of San Diego Historical Society Photograph Collection.)

When he purchased the Stonewall, Waterman also began acquiring land around the mine. In addition to purchasing Lot A from Alfred James and Dr. J. E. Fulton for $75,000 and Lot B from the individuals who had contested Frary and Farley's ownership of the Stonewall for another $75,000, he also purchased Cuyamaca Rancho Lots C, D, E, and F from their owners. Finally, he held in his hands nearly 23,000 acres of contiguous mountain land, about 64% of the acreage that once was Olvera's Cuyamaca Rancho. In time this would become the heart of today's Cuyamaca Rancho State Park. For these extensive land holdings he paid at least $158,000, more than for the two lots where the Stonewall was located. Without stretching the truth too far, it can be said that Robert W. Waterman was a rancher who also owned a lucrative gold mine.

After buying the mine, Robert W. Waterman named his son Waldo superintendent. Bringing his new wife, Myra, Waldo took up residence at the mine. She, however, was gravely ill with tuberculosis, and died five months after the wedding. In 1889 the young widower married Hazel Wood, with whom he had three children. His wife left an interesting collection of letters describing their life together, especially their early years at the mine; the union ended with Waldo Waterman's death in 1903. Most important in recovering the history of the mine during its boom years is the extensive collection of letters from Waldo Waterman to his father in which he described the mine's everyday operation from his post as mine superintendent.

Under Waterman's ownership, his money flowing, the mine entered its most productive years. First of all, under Waldo's supervision, miners sank a three-compartment shaft south of the old mine. (In fact they may have expanded and deepened an existing old shaft.) Probably paid for by Waterman's profits from his silver mines, this shaft provided access to the deeper levels of the lode—the new shaft was the key to exploiting the mine. Eventually, the shaft became more than six hundred feet deep. From the shaft miners cut 3,600 feet of horizontal drifts at six levels to follow the lode, making the Stonewall the deepest and largest mine in the Cuyamacas. Waldo Waterman's plans for increasing the mine's production included erecting an additional twenty-stamp mill that in fact was completed early in 1890, bringing the number of stamps at the mine to thirty.

The Watermans also had new hoist works built to handle the increasing output of ore from the mine. Enclosed and roofed, freshly painted red, rising fifty-six feet, the gallows frame was completed at about the same time as the new mill. For nearly forty years photographers captured its picturesque outline framed in pines against a background of hills. In the immediate vicinity of the hoist and mill stood a blacksmith shop, carpenter shop, mine office, assay office, meeting room, powder house, and other buildings. All in all, Waterman invested an estimated $75,000 in construction at the Stonewall.

Not far from the hoist works was a sawmill that provided fuel for the mine's insatiable boilers which drove two mills and hoisting works and pumps and miscellaneous equipment. It also provided heavy timbers for the mine that were necessary in soft ground. The Watermans sold the sawmill's surplus production to anyone who would buy it.

According to H. John McAleer in *Stonewall Mine and Cuyamaca City* (p. 46) the mill at the Stonewall in 1888 crushed 5,812 tons of ore to produce $198,666 in gold, in 1889 it crushed 8,113 tons of ore worth $216,736, and in 1890 the mine reached its peak production, crushing 22,246 tons of ore worth $344,231.

Estimates vary about how many men worked at the mine during the boom years. McAleer (p. 38) says that in August 1889 the mine employed more than two hundred men, while *The Julian Sentinel* for July 6,1889, asserted that the mine had 130 employees. The California State Mining Bureau's *Report* for 1890 (p. 540) said that in October 1889 the Stonewall employed sixty-five miners and eight mill workers, a total of seventy-three men. Woodcutters, assayers, etc. also labored at the mine. Of course, employment at the mine fluctuated according to need.

Figure 32. The brick reservoir on the knoll above the Stonewall Mine. Another of Waldo Waterman's 1889 improvements, the reservoir stored excellent water piped from today's Azalea spring on Cuyamaca Peak that could be used in the stamp mills or for culinary purposes. In later years the CCC remodeled it to provide water for the Girl Scouts' Camp Tapawingo. Abandoned today.

Perhaps the highest level of employment was in the summer of 1890, the year of peak production. On June 6 that year *The Julian Sentinel* carried this add: "WANTED. MINERS at the Stonewall mine. Ten first-class, A 1 Miners for double hand work in hard rock. None but experienced men need apply. W. S. Waterman, Supt." On August 22, 1890, the newspaper printed the same advertisement, but Waterman now wanted twenty-five miners.

Nine months earlier, late in 1889, the geologist W. A. Goodyear, after visiting the mine, left this description of the lode, presenting a vision of spectacular wealth, the greatest treasure the Cuyamacas ever yielded:

On October 30, 1889, the main shaft at the Stonewall Mine was 400 feet deep, from the bottom of this shaft a level had been driven for some distance in both directions (i.e., northwest and southeast) and some cross cutting had also been done at various points. On the third level north west of the shaft a very large body of ore was exposed for a distance of about 130 feet along the drift with varying thickness, which in places was seen to be more than 20 feet and the face of the drift was still in a very heavy body of quartz. Between the second and third levels the whole of this mass of ore remained almost solid in the mine, very little of it having yet been stoped. But on the second level it is not so extensive nor so large as it is on the third level. From a portion of this body of quartz taken from above the second level, they once made a run of $26,000 in one month, being the best single month's run ever yet made with the present 10 stamp mill....

Almost from the day he bought the Stonewall, Waterman had problems with a neighbor. In September 1886 the newly formed San Diego Flume Co. let a contract for the construction of Cuyamaca Dam immediately north of the mine on land that certainly belonged to Waterman. In October 1887 its promoters belatedly brought suit to condemn Waterman's land where they were building the dam.

In response, Waterman took legal action, asking for a fair price for the land and more than $210,000 in damages. In addition to the loss of grazing and cultivated meadow land, one of his concerns was the possibility of water from the reservoir flooding the Stonewall. Litigation continued until early in 1888 when the governor got far less than he asked for, settling with the Flume Co. for $45,000 and signing over 450 acres to it.

Still, in spite of the wealth the mine produced in the years 1887–1890 and the settlement of the suit with the Flume Co., all was not well with Waterman and the Stonewall Mine. Apparently he had overextended himself in his other enterprises, particularly the San Diego, Cuyamaca, and Eastern Railroad, and needed cash. For this reason, Waterman began to seek a buyer for his Cuyamaca holdings. He found one in the person of a Mr. A. McLaughlin of Chicago, to whom Waterman offered to sell 21,000 acres of land along with between eight hundred and twelve hundred head of cattle, and the Stonewall Mine, all for two million dollars. Because the buyer could not raise the money, negotiations for the purchase collapsed.

In the fall of 1890 a crisis suddenly emerged at the Stonewall. About November it became clear that the supply of high grade ore in the mine was failing. This was only a few months after the mine reached its highest level of production ever, Waldo was attempting to find twenty-five more miners, and the old and new mill were running all their thirty stamps. In addition, the governor was placing great pressures on Waldo to reduce expenses, no doubt because of his financial problems.

On January 18, 1891, Waldo ominously wrote, "Unless we can strike something new there is no more money to be had from Stonewall. I want you to come up soon and see for yourself just how things are and decide what to do."

In 1891 the mine's production fell to $124,848, and in 1892 it reached only $21,582. Still, under Waterman's ownership the Stonewall yielded $1,031,063 in about five years, roughly the same as in the first sixteen years of the mine's history under much less efficient management.

Figure 33. The San Francisco-made twenty-stamp mill at the Stonewall, the largest in the Cuyamacas. The 650-pound stamps were divided into four batteries of five stamps each; they fell only six inches at a rate of 95 to 100 drops per minute. The apron plates were four by nine feet with three drops, as can be seen. Workers dumped pre-crushed ore behind the batteries, and the finely crushed wet pulp made its way down the mercury-covered plates. This new mill operated at full capacity for less than one year, and was shut down completely within five years. (Courtesy of San Diego Historical Society Photograph Collection.)

After Waterman completed his term of office in January 1891, he settled in San Diego, buying a residence that survives today at the intersection of Kalmia and First Streets. As Waldo had requested him to do in January, at the end of March he went to inspect the Stonewall, contracting a cold as the result of a visit to the mountains. The indisposition worsened, became pneumonia, and on April 12, 1891, Robert W. Waterman died. Ironically, the Stonewall, which had yielded a fortune to Waterman, was also the immediate cause of his death.

After he died, his heirs discovered that he had taken out many loans to cover expenses unrelated to the mine, the largest for $120,000 from the Sather Banking Co. of San Francisco that was secured by the Cuyamaca Rancho and the Stonewall Mine. After the settlement of the estate, ownership of these properties passed to the bank.

Why was the Stonewall Mine essentially abandoned with Waterman's death? One theory has it that water, especially from the new reservoir, flooded the mine. But the flow of water in the mine was always under control—even after the dam was completed in 1887 the mine's pumps removed the water efficiently. A much more reasonable explanation is that the mine shut down because its free-milling gold ore was exhausted, just as the ore failed at a certain level in all the Cuyamaca mines.

Sometime in 1891, Waterman's heirs hired a mining engineer, William Miller, to assess the mine's potential production. In his report Miller concluded that gold values in the ore were declining sharply, and he recommended that the owners shut down all but ten of the stamps immediately. The only hope for increased production was to sink the shaft down to a seventh level, a costly procedure that might not result in new discoveries. Given the grave financial problems that came with Waterman's death, this was out of the question. Nor did the new owner, the Sather Banking Co., apparently believe such a venture would be fruitful. Closing the mine seemed prudent. Officially, the mine closed sometime in 1893.

In 1898, five years after the closure of the Stonewall, once more the mine became a center of activity. Workmen from all quarters assembled to begin new operations to profit from the mine's mineral wealth, not from its underground veins but from the tailings that had poured from the two mills and fanned down the slope toward the lake. A Los Angeles company, Strauss and Shinn, bought the Stonewall mill tailings from the Sather Banking Co. and began to process them with cyanide to recover the free gold that had escaped the ancient inefficient amalgamation process.

The cyanide process, discovered late in the 1880s, was simplicity itself. Workers dumped crushed ore, whether fresh from the mill or old tailings, into a weak cyanide solution—poisonous but safe to handle—that was agitated in the presence of air. In theory, every gold atom then combined with the cyanide. In a second stage, the "pregnant liquid" ran through boxes containing zinc shavings that precipitated the gold into a heavy sludge that could be refined and sent directly to the mint.

The first news that the Strauss and Shinn would set up a processing plant appeared in *The San Diego Union* on August 24, 1898. On October 21, the newspaper reported that carpenters were erecting a tank house that measured two hundred by sixty feet. By May 8, 1899, the newspaper said that workers had built a track on which steam-driven cars, apparently loaded by horse-drawn scoops, carried the powdery tailings a few hundred yards from east of the mine to the processing buildings west of the mine. They also erected a temporary dam to prevent the cyanide from poisoning the reservoir.

How long it took to complete the salvage operation is not clear. Nor can writers agree on how much money Strauss and Shinn made from the tailings. A usually reliable source, Harvey Moore, in his *Discovery and History of the Stonewall Jackson Mine,* writes that "Those tailings yielded from $3.00 to $6.00 per ton and a recovery of over $50,000 was made" (p. 2).

Figure 34. The cyanide treatment sheds at the Stonewall, 1898–1899. The abandoned Stonewall is to the right and the reservoir is on the knoll in the center. Barely visible is the steam-driven railroad that brought the tailings over the hill from the mill sites. As can be seen, tailings from the cyanide operation spilled down the slope; a dam supposedly prevented them from reaching Cuyamaca Lake. (Courtesy of San Diego Historical Society Photograph Collection.)

In 1903 promoters made a last attempt to revive the Stonewall. That year the Sather Banking Co. sold the Cuyamaca Rancho along with the Stonewall to a Boston concern for $200,000. To operate the newly founded Cuyamaca Ranch and Mining Co., incorporated at $2,000,000, its owners hired Col. S. H. Lucas of Los Angeles.

Immediately, Lucas began attempts to return the Stonewall to production. With the enthusiasm of a born promoter he told the newspaper that "within thirty days he expected to have a hundred men at work." Six months later he was still clearing the mine, saying that to complete the work he "would secure some miners from the north immediately." In spite of delays that dragged on for more than two years, the new owners did in fact drain the mine and renovate its machinery before a consulting engineer, Mark B. Kerr, whose services they had hired, inspected the Stonewall in October 1905.

Kerr delivered a sanguine report on the mine's condition, asserting that it still held much rich ore. He wrote that "As the well defined gouge on the footwall and the values found on the present bottom of this mine show this to be a deep seated, true fissure vein…there is not a reason from a geological standpoint why the production below the 600-foot level should not be as good as that already explored and stoped above the 600-foot level." In conclusion, he recommended that the owners deepen the shaft to the 1000-foot level with drifts at 100-foot levels.

But to sink that additional four hundred feet of shaft would be expensive. At any rate, Col. Lucas and his backers, although they drained and renovated the Stonewall at what must have been considerable expense, never attempted to deepen the mine. Whether they actually mined any gold at all is very doubtful. The California State Mining Bureau, whose responsibility it was to keep track of such things, wrote in its *Report* in January 1925 that "The mine [the Stonewall] was closed down in 1893 and has been idle since that date" (p. 348).

In 1908 the Sather Banking Co., after foreclosing on the corporation's mortgage, regained possession of the Stonewall. In 1917 it sold the rancho to a Col. A. G. Gassen of San Diego. In turn, his heirs sold it to Mr. and Mrs. Ralph M. Dyar for $200,000 in 1923. It was during the Dyar years that the Stonewall Mine, long abandoned, was razed, its heavy timbers dispersed, and its equipment sold for scrap metal.

Sometime in the year 1926 a writer named Margaret Romer visited Cuyamaca; the result of her visit was an article "The Vanished Cuyamaca" that appeared on p. 36 in *Touring Topics* for August 26. This was the last portrait of the Stonewall before its destruction.

She found very little left of the "ghost town" of Cuyamaca. One end of a long wooden building that she identified as a "200-foot long boarding house" still stood. In fact, this building probably dated from the 1898 cyanide operation. Only two houses remained, one occupied by a caretaker, as well as a few deserted cabins. Other than these survivors, she reported, "the places where the buildings stood are as scars on the ground."

Of the mine's buildings only two very large buildings made of corrugated iron painted red with white window and door frames yet remained. These were the picturesque, nearly forty-year-old hoist and mill, with most of the windows and all the doors broken. Not familiar with mining equipment, this is how she described what she saw upon entering the buildings.

> In another room we see the huge mill of fifteen stamps [actually twenty] and many troughs [usually called plates or aprons] of different sizes to catch the gold as it was washed over them. In still another room we see the large yet finely adjusted scales on which the gold was weighed. Next we come to the room where the shafts go down into the darkness below. A chill creeps over us as we look down into the blackness. We feel the deadly silence. Then we call down and an unnatural voice answers us back. We shiver and move away from the hole. There are the old elevators with the dials indicating the level at which the car stands. [One of these cages is on display at the Stonewall today.] Notice the flat steel

cable [more correctly a belt, some still at the Stonewall site] which holds them. The levers still have the blue calico rags tied around their handles with string so that the operator's hand might not slip—just as he left them when he stopped work years ago.

Within a few years all of this was gone. According to Harvey Moore, it was Ralph M. Dyar's son, Ralph Stearns Dyar, who sold the mine buildings and their contents in 1928 to a Los Angeles salvage company for $500. Many people have regretted the loss of such a splendid monument to Cuyamaca mining history. But, on the other hand, as Romer describes it, the site was hazardous, and no doubt San Diego County was still collecting property taxes on the derelict mine. These are two good reasons for the Dyars to have the mine buildings leveled and its shaft filled in.

The Ranchita Mine. Like the Stonewall Mine, the Ranchita Mine stood well outside the Julian and Banner Mining Districts. It was located at an elevation of 3,400 feet one mile southeast of Banner in Rodriguez Canyon. Through this canyon runs the Elsinore Fault; the Ranchita Mine, unique to Julian mines, in fact lies north of the fault. Weber says (p. 132) that miners worked the Ranchita from its discovery in 1895 to 1899, from 1934 to 1940, and again after the Second World War. Miners sank two shafts with drifts and stopes; one shaft was 330 feet deep. A five-stamp mill, still surviving today rusted and abandoned, worked at the site. For a description of how to visit the Ranchita to view the mill, one of only two in the Cuyamacas, see the Addendum, "Seeing the Cuyamaca Mines Today."

Because it is outside the district, the mine's discovery is not recorded in the *Julian Mining Records*. According to the *Julian Banner,* published in March 1896, a Mexican family named Lopez homesteaded the Ranchita mine site as early as 1870, establishing a small farmstead and running cattle. For twenty-five years the family lived a quiet life on the isolated ranchita until the summer of 1895 when a vaquero named Leandro Woods (otherwise unknown in the records) discovered rich float very near the house. Such were the beginnings of the Ranchita Mine, which eventually produced $150,000 in gold, making it the eighth largest producer in the Cuyamacas.

After the strike, newspapers reported that several parties were interested in purchasing the prospect from Ygnacia Lopez, widowed owner of the property. However, on November 11, 1895, *The San Diego Union* announced that the winner in the competition to buy the mine was Cave Couts, Jr., son of the famous scout and rancher, who paid Mrs. Lopez $5,500 for the property. Couts was best known as the owner of the North County's Guajome Ranch. How a rancher came to buy the Ranchita Mine is not clear, but it is sometimes said that many of the problems at the mine resulted from the fact that its owner

Figure 35. The Ranchita house and mine. This is what happens when someone discovers gold in your back yard—you make a mine there. This view of Rodriguez Canyon facing northeast shows the original Lopez homestead as well as the Ranchita hoist works and mill. All of the buildings have long since disappeared and only some of the durable machinery and waste dumps remain. Lower Banner Canyon is below and to the left. (Courtesy of San Diego Historical Society Photograph Collection.)

lived far away, was not familiar with mining, and did not adequately supervise his property. Perhaps this is true. At any rate, it is certainly true the Ranchita was tangled in years of litigation and had a reputation for mine salting (planting rich ore in a mine to induce a sale) and high grading (miner theft) unequaled by any other Cuyamaca mine.

Miners found substantial amounts of rich ore close to the surface at the Ranchita. As usual, the reports were exaggerated beyond all reason. Two visitors reported that they had seen $200,000 worth of ore at the mine portal, and an anonymous writer in the *Julian Banner* wrote "It will indeed be singular, if the Ranchita does not put Mr. Couts among the gold kings of the world."

Sometime in 1899, Couts sold the mine to the Colorado and California Mineral Development Co. for $120,000. The company's chief owner was Gail Borden, whom the newspaper identified as "the condensed-milk man." The company spent a considerable sum on mine improvements. But the mine's ostensible new owners were stopped in their tracks when a certain Mrs. G. A. Schrader had an injunction served against the Ranchita for $8,300; on March 1, 1900, she had a second injunction served against the company demanding that all work cease at the mine. At this time the newspaper provided the reasons behind this puzzling litigation.

It seems that Mrs. Schrader was Couts' former wife. When they divorced, Couts promised her the sum of $8,000, secured by a mortgage on the Ranchita. When he failed to give her the money, she had taken action against the mine. The outcome of the litigation is not clear, but the mine may have closed down for a time.

Figure 36. The Ranchita's five-stamp mill today. The Rigdon Iron Works of San Francisco made the Ranchita mill in 1896. Once a wooden structure just below the Ranchita's mine collar enclosed the mill, but it has long since disappeared. Now at a regrettably remote location, it would be worth the effort to bring this historic mill to a more public location, such as in Julian, where it would no doubt find many admirers.

But this was nothing compared with what happened next. On April 12, 1900, *The San Diego Union* carried this article.

CHARGED WITH SALTING THE RANCHITA MINE

The Colorado and California Mineral Development company has sued Cave J. Couts of San Diego in the United States circuit court, according to *The Los Angeles Times*. In the complaint filed, the company alleges that on Feb. 3, 1899, it entered into a contract with Couts for the purchase of the Ranchita mine of San Diego, which, according to the plaintiff, Couts represented to be a valuable property, but which turned out, so the company says, to be worthless.

Prior to entering into a contract with the defendant, the company employed George Quigley as an expert to examine the property and report as to the nature and grade of ore. After an examination, so the complaint sets forth, Quigley returned with samples of high grade gold-bearing rock, and declared that the property was worth $120,000, the price asked.

In view of recent disclosures, the company now believes that Quigley was at the time of the examination secretly employed by the defendant, and was a party to the alleged swindle.

By the terms of the contract, Quigley was appointed general manager of the mine, after the company had entered possession of the property. After expending some $11,244.21 in operating the mine, the company came to the conclusion that it had bought a gold brick and not a gold mine.

Several stories have been printed about salting Julian mines for the purpose of making a profitable sale, but this appears to be the only documented evidence for the practice, assuming that the company's accusations were justified. To salt a mine a potential seller would arrange to acquire high grade ore from a producing mine and then introduce it into the mine he was trying to sell, sometimes with the judicious use of a shotgun. In this case, Quigley allegedly misrepresented high grade ore as coming from the Ranchita when it did not.

Years of litigation over the mine began, a period of time, presumably, when the mine was loosely supervised. On May 19, 1903, according to *The San Diego Union,* Couts filed a twenty-one-page bill of exceptions against the company. On September 27, 1903, the paper reported that Couts was filing an appeal against a decision rendered in favor of the plaintiffs, Gail Borden and others. Apparently, the Ranchita's sale to the Colorado and California Mining Development Co. had fallen through. Records show that Couts was once more the owner of the mine after this date.

Helen Ellsberg in her book *Mines of Julian* writes that because the Ranchita was so poorly supervised its miners carried out "systematic high grading." Later she refers to other high graders who brought in "gold dust extracted by mortar and pestle from the rich Ranchito ore they had 'liberated' from the mine." Still later, she speaks of "high graders' extortion" (All quotes are on p. 53). The source of her information was apparently anonymous Julian informants she interviewed before writing her book.

These are rare Julian references to what was a common practice in western mines. Miners everywhere believed that they were entitled to some "family

Figure 37. The Ranchita Mine boiler. Every medium-sized mine had to have a steam engine to power a hoist (if it was a shaft mine), as well as stamp mills, air compressors, pumps, conveyor belts, etc. Sometimes, as in the case of the Stonewall Mine, the steam engine could also drive a sawmill. The fuel for the boiler was always local wood, brought with considerable trouble to the mine site. This Ranchita boiler has rested undisturbed at this site for over a hundred years.

gold" to supplement their wages, and they also knew that no jury would convict them if they were prosecuted. Mine owners understood this also. It seems only reasonable that Julian miners dipped into their employers' mines at times, and particularly at the poorly supervised Ranchita. However, thanks to the fact that Julian gold was very fine, they probably did it on a modest scale. Julian was not Cripple Creek, Colorado, or Goldfield, Nevada, where a miner could carry out a month's wages in his pocket, a lunch pail, or even more wealth in a specially designed harness worn under his clothes. If high grading did in fact blossom in the Julian District, my guess is that it was in the early years when rich surface ore was common.

CHAPTER 7
CONCLUSION

Discoveries of many bodies of extremely rich oxidized ore occurring near or at the surface are not expected in the future.—Geologist Maurice Donnelly, 1934

In the Cuyamaca Mountains outside the Julian-Banner District prospectors made strikes, none of them particularly rich or famous, that nonetheless deserve notice in the region's gold mining history. In general, prospectors made these strikes on the range's perimeter where roof pendants partially circle the Cuyamacas' three peaks.

Boulder Creek Mines. They were located west of Cuyamaca Peak at an elevation of about 2,600 feet where Boulder Creek swings around Mineral Hill before turning straight towards the San Diego River. Here, not far from where today's Boulder Creek Road fords the stream, for more than fifty years the Boulder Creek Mining District flourished in a small way.

For nearly a mile, gold reaches the surface in four zones along the hills north of Boulder Creek. Typical of the district, Julian Schist and quartz diorite enclose the northwest-striking veins holding only small amounts of gold milling out at $6 to $12 a ton. In 1885 prospectors discovered the outcrops and in 1890 the Boulder Creek Gold Mining and Milling Company erected a ten-ton roller mill and other facilities to process the ore. To reach the ore, miners cut three tunnels just north of the creek. Although miners dug several thousand feet of adits in search of profitable ore, little gold came from the mines.

For nearly forty-five years, from 1890 to 1934, George H. Moyer, who lived at Boulder Creek with his family, supervised his Little Giant, the most active mine in the district, as well as other mines located on nine claims close to the road. Further upstream on Mineral Hill were the Boulder Creek and Sixty Two claims. The last mine to close down in the district was the aptly named Last Chance Mine, in 1941.

Figure 38. The Descanso Mine, probably about 1930. The Descanso Mine was located just off Old Viejas Grade not far from the center of Descanso. It had a life of about forty years but never seems to have returned much profit to its owners. As can be seen from this photograph, it was a shaft mine (the shaft is to the right). Today nothing remains to mark the site of the mine. (Courtesy of San Diego Historical Society Photograph Collection.)

Descanso Mines. These mines were located just northwest of the Cleveland National Forest Guard Station near the center of Descanso.

The beginnings of mining at Descanso are not well known, but as early as May 4, 1881, *The San Diego Union* reported that "Charles Ellis [a well-known local rancher] has leased his quartz mine; the new owners are expected to continue the mining operation." What came of this lease is unclear.

The Ellis family continued to labor intermittently at the mine. According to the same paper dated January 1, 1899, Charles Ellis Jr., who had recently been working the mine, had discovered "A fine vein of quartz." A year later, the mine attracted the attention of outside parties. The newspaper on January 1, 1900, reported that "A lead that has been intermittently worked for several years…and from which sixty tons of ore were taken…with a return of some $25 gold per ton, has recently been bonded to eastern parties."

The "eastern parties" may have been a mysterious English group associated with the Descanso mines from the turn of the century to 1940. They included a Major Schute and his wife, Ernestine Sellers, "the English authoress of note," as one newspaper article called her, who leased the mine in the early 1920s to the Suffolk Mining Co. of Los Angeles. They did so under the name of the Descanso Mining Syndicate whose head was A. B. E. White of Brighton, England, "formerly of Descanso."

The *Report* of the State Mining Bureau for 1913–1914 noted that "gold occurs 300 yards west of Descanso where Dr. A. J. MacDougall controls a number of claims including the Magdalena.... Investment work has been carried to a 100 foot shaft." By 1925, according to one account, there were seventeen claims clustered around the original strike, with the Magdalena claim the most active. Here miners sank a 230-foot inclined shaft with drifts in pursuit of the vein.

When the U.S. government raised the price of gold from $20.67 to $35.00 an ounce in the 1930s it stimulated mining in Descanso, as it did in many places. On July 1, 1934, *The San Diego Union* reported that a San Diego syndicate was installing new equipment at the shaft, now 260 feet deep. Work was proceeding on drifts at six levels and a ten-stamp mill had completed its test run. On April 9, 1935, the same paper reported the syndicate under W. W. Crosby "Is said to have produced considerable gold during the last year, but those in charge declined to state the exact amount." A final attempt was made to reactivate the mine in 1940, but the coming of war shut down all gold mines for the duration, and the Descanso mines never revived.

F. Harold Weber's *Geology and Mineral Resources of San Diego County (1963)* succinctly encapsulates the brief life of the Descanso District: "Area first prospected at least as early as the 1880s. Descanso deposit discovered in 1900 and explored sporadically through 1920s. Several thousand dollars of gold and small amount of silver produced during period from 1932 to 1936. Workings inaccessible in 1957" (p. 142).

Pine Hills. The Maude E. prospect, named for the wife of its developer, L. L. Bosworth, was located one mile south of Pine Hills on the slopes above Cedar Creek. The year was 1931. This is the only recorded attempt to find gold in the region of Pine Hills, where outcrops of Julian Schist are common enough.

Of great interest to anyone curious about the history of Cuyamaca mining is the question of how much wealth gold miners took from the range. Unfortunately, no one knows with certainty because no agency, private or governmental, kept production records throughout the district's history. Wells Fargo maintained information in its files, but not all the mines utilized the firm's services, available in Julian as early as 1870. Some mine owners chose to transport their gold privately—the Stonewall Mine was well known for this preference. Some gold the miners sold directly to jewelers or other fabricators. By the 1890s mail service had become so reliable that some mines sent their gold by registered mail directly to the mint at San Francisco, bypassing Wells Fargo and its bookkeepers.

Figure 39. The entrance to the Descanso Mine, dated May 4, 1931. The Descanso Mine was so small that it relied on a bucket to haul men and materials. One of the men is an engineer dressed in fashionable laced boots, broad hat and impractical sport coat, while the other is a miner, about to drop into the mine, wearing serviceable work clothes. The engineer, probably a visitor, carries a modern portable carbide lamp, while the miner wears his lamp on his hard hat to free his hands for labor. (Courtesy of San Diego Historical Society Photograph Collection.)

Donnelly in his 1934 report (p. 352) concluded that "The total production of all mines in the Julian-Banner-Cuyamaca region is believed to be between $4,000,000 and $5,000,000." Weber, writing in 1963 (p. 117), acknowledged Donnelly's estimate, but revised it upwards: "A total of about $5,000,000 [for the district] is estimated by the writer who employed: (1) production figures of the U.S. Bureau of Mines, collected from San Diego County producers since 1890; (2) an interpretation of the extent and nature of workings; and (3) an evaluation of previously published figures (chiefly those of Donnelly, 1934...)." Since Donnelly and Weber based their estimates on what appears to be a wide range of reliable sources, it seems reasonable to respect their production estimates. Let it be said that the Julian District produced $5,000,000, in nineteenth century dollars, in gold.

On the same page Donnelly lists the most productive mines in the Cuyamacas:

Stonewall	$2,000,000
Golden Chariot	700,000
Ready Relief	500,000
Helvetia	450,000
Owens	450,000
Blue Hill or Gardiner	200,000
North Hubbard	200,000
Ranchita	150,000

In addition, fifteen mines produced between $25,000 and $50,000 each: Antelope, Chaparral, Cincinnati Belle, Eagle, Elevada, Hidden Treasure, High Peak, Kentuck S., Madden, Redman, San Diego, Shamrock, Van Wert, Warlock, and Washington.

Sixteen mines probably produced less than $25,000: Cable, Chieftain, Eldorado, Ella, Fraction, Gold King, Gold Queen, Granite Mountain, Hidden Treasure [also listed above], Homestake, Neptune, North Star, Oriflamme, Padlock, Ruby, South Hubbard, and Tom Scott.

How much of California's gold did the Cuyamacas yield? According to one well-known authority, Mary Hill, California has produced $2,324,000,000 in gold at $20.00 an ounce. The $5,000,000 contribution the Cuyamacas made to this sum was less than one-half of one percent, or .22%, to be more exact. However, because the price paid for gold was so unstable and much gold was marketed without records, the figure cannot be precise. Perhaps the most reasonable conclusion is that the Cuyamacas produced substantially less than one half of one percent of California's gold.

Some individuals have written that the district's production would have been higher if two misfortunes had not beset the Julian mines. The first of these was the Cuyamaca Rancho claims that required mine owners to spend money on litigation that should have gone into developing the mines. Certainly this was true, but the mines seem to have recovered nicely after the courts rejected the claims—perhaps it would be better to say that the rancho claims retarded mine development, but in the long run they probably did not reduce gold production significantly.

The other misfortune, so the theory goes, was prejudice against the district from two sources that curtailed crucial outside investments in the mines. This theory holds that northern California investors refused to put money into southern California mines such as those at Julian. Also, it's said that Julian mines suffered because Union-minded San Diego business leaders were biased against former Confederate mine owners conspicuous in Julian.

The theory that northern California financiers would not invest in the south is mentioned in only a few sources, and it is impossible to verify. Certainly the Civil War left a residue of bad feeling, but it's impossible to find even one example where outsiders denied investments in the Julian mines because some mine owners were southerners. After all, non-southerners controlled many of the largest mines such as the Owens, Golden Chariot, Helvetia and Stonewall (Jackson), in spite of its name. San Diego merchants and lawyers quickly sprang into the breach to defend the mines against the rancho claims.

If investors believed money could be made in the Cuyamaca mines they would have spent their money to develop them regardless of the fact that the mines were located in southern California or that some mine owners were former rebels. In modern economic life the profit motive trumps all other cards. No, it's fair to say that the determining factor in Cuyamaca gold production was how much gold miners found in the quartz, and the rancho claims and possible outside prejudice against the Cuyamaca mining districts meant little, if anything at all.

Does mining in the Cuyamacas have a future? Needless to say, writers on the subject have voiced differing opinions, from unbridled optimism to more than a little skepticism. Of these commentators, it was Maurice Donnelly, geologist and author of *Geology and Mineral Deposits of the Julian District,* (1934) who made the most provocative, and encouraging, comments on the subject. In his report Donnelly assumed the district did indeed have a future, and he made a number of recommendations how best to revive the Cuyamaca gold mines (pp. 369–370).

To the question of new discoveries he gave a qualified answer: "Discoveries of many bodies of extremely rich, oxidized ore occurring near or at the surface are not expected in the future." This statement implies that prospectors would make not many, but *some* such discoveries. Then he added, "Even after the long period of time during which the Julian gold deposits have been known, it can not be said that all of the favorable ground has been intelligently prospected." In other words, perhaps prospectors have just not looked hard enough. He recommended that "areas depicted on the map as representing schistose rocks should be well prospected."

Figure 40. Single-jack drilling contest at Julian, 1902. The miner, working alone, has a certain period of time, usually 15 minutes, to see how deep he can drill in hard rock. Note how he has carefully laid out a supply of graduated drills, from large to small. To ensure he has sharp drills, he will change them often, and he will use a decreasing size so that the drill does not stick in the hole, a sure way to lose the contest. (Courtesy of Julian Pioneer Museum.)

Speaking words that no doubt sent a thrill through the heart of every Julian miner, he wrote "The ore zone may be expected to extend in depth considerably beyond any point attained by previous mining operations in the district." But he warned, "Ores mined in the future will probably contain less free gold and more auriferous sulphides and gold compounds than was the case during the previous history of the camp. Such ore can not be treated economically by amalgamation only. Everything considered, flotation [placing ore in water with soap-like chemicals to float off unwanted material] in some form offers the best possibility for a high recovery of gold." This suggests that the key to the revival of Cuyamaca underground mining might very well rest in improved technology to deal with deeper and more complex ores.

No doubt having in mind that Cuyamaca gold was fine, and therefore almost invisible, he recommended frequent assaying, saying that panning to test for gold, a common practice, could be misleading (Waldo Waterman also often made this recommendation in his letters to his father). He added what appears to be a warning about the threat of high grading that suggests that the practice may have been more of a problem in the district than has been suspected: "The richness of some of the ore makes necessary careful mining extraction *to avoid losses*. Sacking in stopes *under supervision* may be advisable [my emphases.]" Perhaps the Ranchita, with its reputation for high grading, may not have been so unusual in the district after all.

The future, Donnelly thought, lay in exploiting the district's deeper and more complex ores. Since the time of his writing, however, no one has seen fit to undertake the admittedly expensive extraction and treatment of such gold ore. Nor, as he predicted, have prospectors found any new deposits of rich oxidized surface ore. The discovery of the Ranchita Mine, nearly 110 years ago, was the district's swan song.

Recent decades have seen the introduction of a new revolutionary method of gold extraction. Called heap leaching, it requires excavating vast amounts of rock containing low-grade gold, depositing it on pads to prevent pollution, and then pouring a weak cyanide solution over the heap. The cyanide, now containing gold in solution, is retrieved and refined. While U.S. leach heap mines are most numerous in northern Nevada, in 1988 California had fifteen such mines. Imperial County has several leach heap mines.

Some have suggested that such a mine might be feasible in the Julian District, but there are great obstacles to developing such a mine. Heap leaching is only feasible with large amounts of rock which, presumably, earthmovers would excavate from the mineralized belt southeast of Julian, now an area with some homes and scenic roads. The enormous and unattractive leach heap with its deadly cyanide would have to rise somewhere in the lower Banner area, I assume, at an unavoidably conspicuous site. And of course, there is the problem of finding an adequate source of water in the dry Cuyamaca rain shadow. For environmental, economic, and above all, political reasons it seems highly unlikely that a Cuyamaca leach heap mine will ever become a reality.

Finally, a word should be said about how the discovery of gold affected the history of the region. No doubt at all, the discovery had an immediate and

Figure 41. Drilling stone at Julian. This block of stone remains today at the Julian Pioneer Museum, a survivor of the drilling contests that were held in the town. Note that the miners went to the effort of bringing this block of hardest granite from out of town to serve as a challenge for the contestants. On the Fourth of July, drilling contests were popular in mining towns all over the west, including Julian. The stone serves to-day as a fitting memorial to Julian's colorful mining days, and its hard-working miners.

powerful effect on the economy and people of the mountains. It pumped $5,000,000 in nineteenth century dollars into the local economy, attracting many people from many different states and foreign countries who would not have come to the mountains without the wealth that the mines delivered, wheth-er they were miners or storekeepers and others or their dependents. Without this wealth the town of Julian would have been only a small market center— a general store or two, a blacksmith shop, a saloon—that met the needs of local farmers, perhaps something like nineteenth century Descanso. The dis-covery of gold was also a bonanza to Cuyamaca ranchers and farmers who brought food to Julian's tables. Beyond the mountains the income from gold benefited the whole region.

In the place of rough horse trails, the mines brought better roads across the range from the coast to the desert and a heavily traveled route parallel with the range from Descanso to Julian. Mine owners built secondary access roads that led to their mines, especially in the rugged hills above Banner. Many of them survive today.

Mining claims altered the land ownership pattern in the area. A glance at a map shows large tracts of private land in the northern part of the range that date from the district's mining days. Had miners not made their claims, the amount of public land would have been much larger in the northern Cuyamacas.

But aside from these immediate economic and social changes, the discovery of gold brought something intangible that has grown in importance with the passage of time and the arrival of the tourist in his automobile. Gold gave us the time when promoters worked their wiles on investors, when young miners sweated hard underground and fought it out in the street in front of the saloon, when new schoolmarms were quickly taken in marriage by locals, when wagonloads of rich ore rolled to the stamps whose pounding deafened their neighbors, when miners died tragically in cave-ins, and families grew up remembering forever the stories their fathers told about the glorious spring of '70 when a poor man in this good camp, because the gold lay close to the surface, might find a treasure.

Today we can see that unknowingly the pioneers were building the foundation for the prosperity that the late twentieth century has brought to the region, but especially the town of Julian. Many visitors come to the picturesque village to see historic buildings from its heroic age, to tour its mines, to glance down its nineteenth century streets, and while they are in the town, buy a souvenir, a warm cap and gloves, an apple pie, a light lunch, or even decide on a weekend in a bed and breakfast, the better to savor the town's special atmosphere that its mining past created.

It seems unlikely that tourists would come in such numbers today if Julian was only a century-old farm town with its history rooted in the mundane facts of agriculture and not in mining's spectacular booms, busts, and hidden treasures. More than a century after the first strike, the romance of mining and money-making meet mostly harmoniously in Julian, creating a new source of wealth for the townspeople. Julian tourism, based on the golden glories of the mining past, has yielded, and for the foreseeable future will continue to yield, much greater dividends than all the Julian mines in all their 130 years.

ADDENDUM
SEEING THE CUYAMACA MINES
TODAY

The best place to begin a tour to see what remains of the Cuyamaca mines is the Julian Pioneer Museum on Washington Street near the town's Main Street. Housed in a former blacksmith shop and one-time brewery, for nearly fifty years the museum has collected mementos from the town's first days, such as mining equipment, family portraits of early miners, mining photographs, and other memorabilia. Emphasizing prospecting and placer mining, an instructive video that runs much of the time displays scenes of old time gold mining, for the most part in northern California. A half hour spent looking over the collections provides an excellent introduction to what early Cuyamaca mining was all about.

Directly in front of the museum stands a granite boulder with conspicuous drilling holes. In Julian's early days miners hauled the rock here to provide a location for Fourth of July drilling contests. In a given period of time (usually fifteen minutes), a miner, competing with others, attempted to hand drill into this rock as deeply as possible, the deepest hole winning the contest.

After leaving the museum, the visitor may walk a short block to Main Street and turn left to pass by the modest clapboard Drury Bailey house, completed in 1876, probably the oldest structure in town.

Just past the Bailey house is the entrance to the Julian cemetery. After climbing up the hill on generous steps the visitor has an excellent view into the town that Drury Bailey had first surveyed in April 1870. Buried in the cemetery are many individuals mentioned in this book including members of the Bailey family.

To see what remains of the gold mines that once blanketed Gold Hill above the town, drive to C Street (it crosses Main Street) at the center of town. Turn left (east) to follow the signs up the hill to enter the parking lot for the Eagle-High Peak Mine a few minutes later. This is the only Cuyamaca mine open to the public that survives in good condition.

For a modest fee, informed guides lead a quarter-mile tours through the mine, one of only two authentic mine tours in southern California (the other is at the Tropico Mine near Mojave), entering at the Eagle Mine and emerging from the High Peak Mine on the far side of Gold Hill. The mostly level well-lighted tour takes about an hour and provides a painless introduction to underground mining. Visitors return by way of a walk through the woods to the parking lot where they can visit a small museum with a gem collection and vintage photographs. On the hill above the parking lot visitors can admire the twenty-two-ton, San Francisco-made five-stamp mill that has been at the mine since 1872, as well as a small one-stamp mill. Guides also demonstrate gold panning. Tours of the mine are available just about every day, but sometimes they are not offered thanks to bad weather and other compelling reasons. For confirmation call ahead to the Eagle Mining Co. Highly recommended.

After leaving the mine parking lot, turn right and watch for a sign "Washington Mine" on a short spur to the left. Park your car and walk about five hundred feet to see an open building containing early mining equipment such as smelting furnaces, sluice boxes and hand-turned ore mills. Nearby is a plaque informing the visitor that the Julian Historical Society dedicated this site in 1969 to commemorate the discovery of the George Washington Mine on February 22, 1870. Easily overlooked is a small fenced arrastra below the open building with a plaque dedicated to former owners of the mine. A forty-yard walk will take visitors to what is left of the mine's original tunnel, now partially collapsed and firmly locked. One hundred thirty years ago this is where Cuyamaca hard rock mining began. The return route to Julian is down C Street.

To visit what is left of the largest Cuyamaca mine, the Stonewall, drive to Cuyamaca Rancho State Park. On the main road through the park, Highway 79, midway between Paso Picacho Campground and Lake Cuyamaca watch for the well-marked paved spur to the east that leads through pleasant meadows to a parking lot on the hillock above the lake.

The fenced area at the original hoist building and three-compartment shaft now encloses some early equipment: a man car or cage, remains of smoke stacks, fragments of the 600-foot belts used in the shaft, two large wheels (or speaves) over which the belts passed, as well as several ore large buckets, rounded so they would not catch on the walls of the shaft. In such a bucket as this the hapless reporter made his 270-foot drop into the Owens Mine, as described in Chapter 3. Just north of the fenced area is the massive foundation of the twenty-stamp mill the Watermans completed in February 1890, while high on the knoll to the west is the fenced Waterman hexagonal brick reservoir, much remodeled.

The original mine shaft and old ten-stamp mill were located about four hundred feet northeast of the Waterman shaft. Only collapsed ground marks the old site; probably Charles Hensley made his original strike close to this location. Mill tailings from both the old and the new mills spilled down this slope towards the lake, while the waste dumps and cyanide reclamation buildings were west of the Waterman shaft, their locations now overgrown with large pines.

Up the hill to the east is a small museum dedicated in 1980, containing excellent enlarged photographs of the Stonewall Mine, as well as some explanatory text.

At the K.Q. Recreational Vehicle Ranch, once the site of the Gold King and Gold Queen Mines, Bob Atkins has collected some early mining and assaying equipment that he has assembled in a small museum. Especially notable are two miners' scales originally used to weigh gold. Located at a well-marked exit opposite Harrison Park Road midway between Cuyamaca Rancho State Park and Julian on Highway 78, the ranch is private, and the visitor who wishes to visit the museum should call ahead or ask at the gate.

A short drive from Julian and a one-hour walk will take the visitor to the abandoned Warlock Mine on the steep western slope above Banner Canyon, the site of many early mines now lost in chaparral and rockslides. Drive east of Julian one mile, turn right on Whispering Pines Road and then immediately right again, turn left on marked Woodland Road and left again a half a mile later for a brief distance until the concrete ends. Park off the road and follow the trail down the steep canyon to the east.

This is the historic Banner Mine Road, a route between Julian and Banner from about 1890 to 1925 when Highway 78 was completed to the desert. A mile's walk on the badly eroded trail that drops about seven hundred feet in altitude will take the visitor to the Warlock, which is clearly visible from the trail. Along the way on the right is a short blocked mine tunnel, possibly part of the Golden Gem mines.

Most of them collapsed, the Warlock buildings are in bad condition. They include several residences, a supervisor's office building, a mill, and a towering postmodern metal treatment plant, survivors of the last attempt to revive the mine in the 1950s. All equipment is gone from the mine, and the tunnel is locked shut. Private property blocks the trail at this point so the visitor must return up the trail to his car. Be advised that the round trip requires about two hours of walking and no water is available on the trail.

If a curious mining enthusiast has a high-clearance vehicle (four-wheel drive is not needed) and is not rattled by rough roads, he can make a short driving excursion to see what remains of two notable Banner mines, the Ranchita and the Golden Chariot. To visit the mine sites and return to the highway requires about two hours of slow driving.

Chariot Canyon Road, the starting point, begins opposite the Banner Store, at 2,600 foot elevation on Highway 78 five miles east of Julian. The name of the road is misleading, since Chariot Canyon is actually a short distance to the west, but the road will enter the upper reaches of the canyon in about two miles. Drive up steep rocky Chariot Canyon Road for 1.3 miles until a junction with a road to the left, or east, appears. Take this, the unmarked Rodriguez Spur Truck Trail on the U.S.G.S. Julian Quadrangle, for one level mile to see the Ranchita Mine dumps and impressive abandoned five-stamp mill set in green meadows. Unfortunately, the property is posted and the visitor must be satisfied with distant views and photographs, but the site is impressive. After seeing the Ranchita, turn around and return to Chariot Canyon Road. (At the present time the continuation of the Rodriguez Spur Truck Trail into Anza-Borrego Desert State Park is impassable for four-wheel vehicles.)

Continue driving a steep one-half mile up Chariot Canyon Road to the saddle at 3,400 feet with a view of Banner Canyon behind and the Golden Chariot Mine about a half mile ahead. This, the largest Banner mine, consists of a cluster of new, well-maintained buildings prominently marked with no trespassing signs, so the visitor must be satisfied with an inspection of the mine site from the road only. The mine stands on a kind of a terrace just below the road in expansive Chariot Canyon, with Chariot Creek plunging into a steep gorge to the west that leads to the site of the Hubbard, Ready Relief, and Redman Mines far below, and then crossing eventually under Highway 78. After passing and inspecting the buildings of the Golden Chariot, find a convenient place to turn around and return down Chariot Canyon Road back to the Banner Store.

The adventurous driver in his high-clearance vehicle may want to continue straight ahead up Chariot Canyon Road to join the Mason Valley Truck Trail at about 4,000 foot elevation. This rocky curving road drops eastward very steeply down Oriflamme Canyon to reach, eventually, Highway S-2 near Box Canyon. This is about fifteen miles from the starting point at the Banner store. Along this road the traveler will see a lonely chaparral and desert landscape, but unfortunately, no mines. Once there were small tunnels all along Chariot Canyon Road, but they have collapsed and chaparral conceals the places where many miners once had such high hopes of finding a fortune.

NOTES

Chapter 1   Where the Gold Came From

Page 1   The epigraph is from *The Peninsular Ranges,* p. 70. Many books have theorized on the origins of precious metals, but most of them are written for specialists who have knowledge of geology, mineralogy, and chemistry. For a good explanation of the origins of precious metals near batholiths that is written for the layman see Jeffrey St. John and the Editors of Time Life Books, *Noble Metals,* especially pp. 76–77. Essential, of course, for an understanding of the origins of Cuyamaca gold is Michael J. Walawender's *The Peninsular Ranges.*

Chapter 2   Gold in the Cuyamacas!

Page 7   "diary for that year." The diary is at S. D. Historical Society Archives.

Page 7   "San Diego businessman, Joshua Sloane." Rensch, *Chronology* p. 2, and Smythe, *History,* pp. 288–289.

Page 7   "but also owned Cuyamaca ranchland." Smythe, *History,* pp. 278–279.

Page 8   "become the Julian Mining District." The sources for information on the gold discovery, sometimes questionable, are Dan Forrest Taylor, *Julian Gold,* ms. at Julian High School with a copy at S. D. Historical Society Archives; Horace Fenton Wilcox's *How Gold Was Discovered at Julian,* ms. at the S. D. Public Library; *The Julian Banner,* March 1896, at S. D. Historical Society Archives; early issues of the *S. D. Union;* and Myrtle Botts, *History of Julian.* By far the best general source of information on Julian's early mining history is Gale W. Sheldon's *Julian Gold Mining Days,* M. A. Thesis, Dept. of History, San Diego State University, 1959.

Page 8   "well into the twentieth century." For the backgrounds of these Georgians see LeMenager, *Julian City,* pp. 43–58.

Page 8   "referred to as A. H. Coleman." Two articles that appeared in the single issue *Julian Banner* (March 1896) which do not always agree in detail but tell substantially the same story, apparently first gave credit to Drury Bailey and Michael Julian as the discoverers of Julian gold. L. Newton Bailey, not related to the founders of Julian, wrote one article for the paper, entitled "Ye Old Pioneers" while James A. Jasper, newspaper man, constable, county supervisor, and historian may have written the other; this unsigned article bears the title "Julian District. Its Location and History…" Bailey wrote, "In the winter of 1870 gold was first discovered in the Julian district by D. D. Bailey and Mike Julian." The location, he says, was on a flat east of town where the cousins successfully panned gold. The anonymous article agrees, but dates the event to between January 1 and 10, 1870. Then, Bailey writes, "About the 1st of February Elza Wood and Coleman" found gold in Coleman Creek (Elza Wood has never been adequately identified.) The anonymous article says "A man by the name of Coleman discovered placer gold in the creek south of Julian in January 1870," presumably after Bailey and Julian made their discovery. However, these articles were written more than twenty years after the event, and so do not carry the weight of the 1870 *San Diego Union* articles that give Frederick Coleman credit for the discovery.

Page 16   "very high praise indeed." Quoted in Sheldon, *Julian Gold,* pp. 36–37.

Chapter 3   The Mines Flourish, the Mines Are Threatened

Page 18   "a gloomy place to work…." Morse, "A Trip to the Mines," p. 16.

Page 18   "between $25,000 and $50,000." Weber, *Geology,* p. 166, and Donnelly, *Geology,* p. 352.

Page 20   "victim of internal injuries." *S. D. Union,* Jan. 10 and 13, 1906.

Page 22   "picking and pounding the treasure." Quoted in Sheldon, *Julian Gold*, pp. 76–77.

Page 23   "unusual metals for the Julian district." Weber, *Geology,* p. 131.

Page 24   "260 feet southeast and 200 feet northwest." Calif. State Min. Bur. *Rept.,* VI, 1886, p. 87.

Page 25   "dearly in transportation expenses." Sheldon, *Julian Gold,* p. 253.

Page 25   "at $100.00 each." *S. D. Union,* May 15, 1874.

Page 25   "with a boarding house nearby." Calif. State Min. Bur. *Rept.* IX, 1890, p. 146.

Page 25   "Denverite, Egbert B. Moore." Sheldon, *Julian Gold*, p. 253.

Page 26   "plant never went into operation." Ibid., p. 255.

Page 27   "were well within the rancho." See Ibid., pp. 88–128, and R. Martin, "Cuyamaca Land Grant Trial," for general information on the case.

Page 27   "both in San Francisco and San Diego." For information about Luco see Crane, "The Pueblo Lands," pp. 119–124, and Pourade, *History of S. D.,* IV, p. 91.

Page 27   "Cuyamaca Rancho over the mines." The best source of information on these arguments, and the counter-arguments, is St. Clair

Denver's brief defending the miners' position that the *S. D.Union* published from Sept. 9 through Sept. 16, 1873.

Page 28 "might hang the claimants' case." R. Martin, "Cuyamaca Land Grant Trial." p.13, and Hayes, *Julian Mines,* p. 36. The Spanish text is in Hayes, p. 136.

Page 29 "enterprise of honest men" Ellsberg, *Mines,* pp. 20–21. Date not given.

Page 29 "within Cuyamaca Rancho." A copy of the Pascoe report is at the museum in Cuyamaca Rancho State Park.

Page 31 "asked to leave the district." Sheldon, *Julian Gold,* p. 119.

Chapter 4 Banner and Beyond

Page 33 "the heading about three feet." Young, *Black Powder,* p. 18.

Page 35 "brought about sixteen dollars." Sheldon, *Julian Gold,* p. 208, quoting Calif. State Min. Bur. *Report,* VI, 1886, p. 86.

Page 36 " 'panned from other ores.' " Botts, *History,* p. 11.

Page 37 "and panned out $28." Taylor, *Julian Gold,* p. 11.

Page 38 "at work in the Julian district." Sheldon, *Julian Gold,* p. 208.

Page 42 "and sold it to Denver interests." Ibid., pp. 212–222.

Page 42 "according to Sheldon." Ibid., p. 221.

Page 42 "and $673,000 in 1898." The production figures are from California. Division of Mines, *Bulletin 122,* pp. 236–238, quoted in Sheldon, *Julian Gold,* Appendix A.

Chapter 5 Banner's Best Mines

Page 46 "from the mine tunnels...above." Sheldon, *Julian Gold,* p. 147.

Page 46 "a new stage in its history." Ibid.

Page 47 "the largest mines in the district." Weber, *Geology,* pp. 132–133.

Page 48 " 'sugar quartz' common to the area." Walawender, *Penin. Ranges,* pp. 72–74.

Page 49 "the mine's first days." Botts, *Hist. of Julian.* pp. 9–10.

Page 50 "returned them...$6,000." Botts, *Hist. of Julian,* p.11.

Page 50 "King sold out to his partners for $25,000." *S.D.Union,* Jan. 26, 1873.

Page 50 "holding most of the shares." *S.D.Union,* Nov. 9, 1873.

Page 50 "$90,000 in gold coin from its owners." Weber, in his *Geology,* p. 124, says they were James and Alex McDonald.

Page 50 "typical of most Julian mines." Weber. *Geology,* pp. 124–126.

Page 50 "significant gold production is not clear." Kofron, *Age and Origin...*p. 15.

Page 52 "a thousand feet of workings." Weber, *Geology,* p. 133.

Page 53 "was done from 1888 to 1900." Ibid., p. 146.

Page 53 "bought out the Gold King Mining Co." *S. D. Sun,* Feb. 25, 1896.

Page 54 "the Gardiner Tunnel, and others." Weber, *Geology,* p. 127.

Page 55 "while no. 3 was established in 1957." Ibid., pp. 126–127.

Page 57 "but apparently little ore was removed." Ibid., p. 135.

Chapter 6   The Stonewall and Ranchita Mines

Page 59 "mine structures razed in the late 1920s." In 1986 H. John McAleer of the California State Dept. of Parks and Recreation produced an excellent history of the Stonewall Mine and Cuyamaca, *Stonewall Mine and Cuyamaca City.* I have employed it as the major source for this chapter.

Page 59 "as discoverers of the mine." Sheldon, *Julian Gold,* p. 224, and McAleer, *Stonewall Mine,* pp. 11–12.

Page 61 "discovered the Stonewall Mine." See George Hensley's biography in Van Dyke's *City and County of S.D.,* pp. 118–119.

Page 61 "or so the story goes." Moore, *The Discovery...* p. 2, Botts, *History...* p. 49, among others.

Page 61 "to do with the mine." Rensch, *Chronology...* p. 15.

Page 63 "where Charles Hensley first discovered it." Weber, *Geology,* pp. 133, 135.

Page 64 "covered the engine and batteries." McAleer, *Stonewall Mine,* p. 15.

Page 66 "making the mine profitable." As the primary source of information concerning Waterman, I have relied on Alexandra Helen Luberski's study, *Robert W. Waterman, 1887–1891: California's Forgotten Progressive.* M. A. Thesis, History Dept. San Diego State University, 1984.

Page 67 " 'the mine will last for years.' " Quoted in McAleer, *Stonewall Mine,* p. 32.

Page 69 "Waterman's death in 1903." For Hazel Waterman, see S. B. Thornton, *Daring to Dream.*

Page 69 "post as mine superintendent." My thanks go to Thomas Crandall, who made his materials on the correspondence available to me.

Page 71 "with the present 10 stamp mill..." Calif. State Min. Bur., *Report IX, 1890,* p. 143.

Page 72 "flooded the mine." Botts, *History...* p. 18.

Page 73 "sent directly to the mint." Young, *Western Mining,* pp. 283–285.

Page 74 "a Boston concern for $200,000." *S. D. Union,* Jan. 11, 1903.

Page 74 " 'a hundred men at work.' " Ibid.

Page 74 " 'miners from the north immediately.' " *S. D. Union,* June 11, 1903.

Page 75 " 'above the 600-foot level.' " Kerr, *Report*...p. 4. Sheldon had access to George H. Clark's *Engineer's Report on the Stonewall Mine.* See Sheldon, *Julian Gold,* p. 269. It is now lost.

Page 75 "for $200,000 in 1923." Although sometimes it is said that he had a partner in the enterprise, only Ralph Dyar's name appears on the deed. S. D. Co. *Deed Book 958,* p. 204.

Page 75 "Only two houses remained." Alfred Lewis, a turkey farmer who became the Cuyamaca dam caretaker, moved the governor's house to his land about a mile north of the lake where it still survives. See the interview with H. M. Moore, Feb. 8, 1974, p. 82.

Page 76 "According to Harvey Moore." Interview with H. M. Moore, Feb. 8, 1974, pp. 22–23.

Page 76 "eighth largest producer in the Cuyamacas." Donnelly, *Geology,* p. 352.

Page 77 "$200,000 worth of ore at the mine portal." *S. D. Sun,* Oct. 2, 1896.

Page 77 "a considerable sum on mine improvements." *S. D. Union,* Nov. 20, 1899.

Chapter 7 Conclusion

Page 81 "little gold came from the mines." Weber, *Geology,* p. 123.

Page 81 "the aptly named Last Chance Mine, in 1941." See my essay "Our Very Own Mining District" in *A Year in the Cuyamacas,* pp. 126–129.

Page 82 "the Suffolk Mining Co. of Los Angeles." Friends… *Descanso, Place*...p. 30.

Page 83 " 'formerly of Descanso.' " *S. D. Union,* Aug. 3, 1940.

Page 83 "with drifts in pursuit of the vein." Weber, *Geology,* p. 140.

Page 83 "outcrops of Julian Schist are common enough." Ibid., p. 155.

Page 85 "one half of one percent of California's gold." Hill, *Gold,* p. 266.

Page 88 "California had fifteen such mines." Hill, *Gold,* p. 228

Page 88 "might be feasible in the Julian district." S. D. Assoc. of Geologists, Introduction to *Selected Geological and Historical Aspects of the Julian Gold Mining District, 1987.*

SOURCES CITED

Newspapers: *The San Diego Union, San Diego Sun, Julian Sentinel.*

Bailey, L. Newton. "Ye Old Pioneers, A Historical Sketch," *Julian Banner. Single Edition, March 1896.* p. 1.

Botts, Myrtle. *History of Julian.* (Julian: Julian Hist. Soc., 1969).

California. State Mining Bureau. *Reports.* 1886+.

Crane, Clare B. "The Pueblo Lands: San Diego's Hispanic Heritage," *Jour. of S.D. History,* XXXVII, no. 2, (Spring, 1991) pp. 105–127.

Donnelly, Maurice. "Geology and Mineral Deposits of the Julian District" *Calif. Jour. of Mines and Geology,* 30, (1934) pp. 331–370.

Ellsberg, Helen. *Mines of Julian.* (Glendale: La Siesta Press, 1972).

Fetzer, Leland. *A Year in the Cuyamacas.* (S.D.: Tecolote Pubs., 1998).

Friends of the Descanso Library. *Descanso Place of Rest.* (S.D.: Tecolote Pubs., 1988).

Hayes, Benjamin J. *The Julian Mines. Exceptions to the Survey of the Cuyamaca Grant. Before the Surveyor General of California.* (S. F.: A. L. Bancroft and Co., 1873).

Hill, Mary. *Gold. The California Story.* (Berkeley: U. C. Press, 1999).

Jasper, James A. (?) "Julian District. Its Location and History, Mines and Towns." *Julian Banner. Single Edition, March 1896.* p. 1.

Julian Banner, March 1896. Single Issue.

Julian Mining Records. At S.D. Historical Society Archives.

Kerr, Mark B. *Report on the Stonewall Mine, 1905.* ms. at S.D. Historical Society Archives.

Kofron, Ronald J. *Age and Origin of Gold Mineralization in the Southern Portion of the Julian Mining District.* M. S. Thesis, Geology Dept., S.D. State University, 1984.

LeMenager, Charles R. *Julian City and Cuyamaca Country.* (Ramona: Eagle Peak Pub. Co., 1992).

Luberski, Alexandra. *Governor Robert Whitney Waterman, 1887–1891.* M. A. Thesis, History Dept. S.D. State University, 1984.

Martin, Richard C. "Cuyamaca Land Grant Trial." *Jour. of S.D. History,* XVII, no. 1 (Winter, 1971) pp. 3–13.

McAleer, H. John. *Stonewall Mine and Cuyamaca City.* (Sacramento: Calif. Dept. of Parks and Recreation, 1986).

Miller, William. *Descriptive Report of the Stonewall Mine.* ms. 1892 (?), Bancroft Library.

Moore, Harvey M. *The Discovery and History of the Stonewall Jackson Mine.* ms.

——————. Interview, Feb. 8, 1974. At Calif. Dept. of Parks and Recreation. S.D. Headquarters.

Morse, Mary, "A Trip to the Mines," *Jour. of S.D. History,* XIII, no. 1, (Jan. 1967) pp. 8–18.

Pourade, Richard F. *History of San Diego,* 7 vols, (S.D.: Union-Tribune Pub. Co., 1960–1977).

Rensch, Hero Eugene. *Chronology of the Stonewall Mine.* (State of California, Cuyamaca Rancho State Park, 1953).

San Diego Association of Geologists. *Selected Geological and Historical Aspects of the Julian Gold Mining District, 1987.*

Sheldon, Gale M. *Julian Gold Mining Days.* M. A. Thesis, History Dept., S.D. State University, 1959.

Smythe, William E. *History of San Diego.* (S.D.: History Co., 1908).

St. John, Jeffrey and the Editors of Time-Life Books. *Noble Metals.* (Alexandria, Va.: Time-Life Books, 1984).

Taylor, Dan Forrest. *Julian Gold.* ms. Copy at S.D. Historical Society Archives.

Thornton, Sally Bullard. *Daring to Dream.* (S.D.: S.D. Historical Society, 1987).

U.S. Bureau of the Census. Census Reports for Julian District, 1870, 1880, and 1900. At S.D. Historical Society Archives.

Van Dyke, Theodore S. *City and County of San Diego.* (S.D.: Leberthon & Taylor, 1888).

Walawender, Michael J. *The Peninsular Ranges.* (Dubuque: Kendall/Hall, 2000).

Waterman, Waldo. *Report of the Stonewall Mine and Cuyamaca Ranch,* ms., Sept. 22, 1891. Bancroft Library.

Weber, F. Harold. *Geology and Mineral Resources of San Diego County.* County Report 3. (S. F.: Calif. Div. of Mines, 1963).

Wilcox, Horace Fenton. *How the Julian Mines Were Discovered.* Ms. S.D. Public Library.

Young, Otis E. *Black Powder and Steel.* (Norman: U. of Oklahoma Press, 1976).

——————. *Western Mining: An Informal Account of Precious-Metals Prospecting, Lode Mining, and Milling on the American Frontier from Spanish Times to 1893.* (Norman: U. of Oklahoma Press, 1970).

INDEX

SUNBELT PUBLICATIONS

"Adventures in the Natural and Cultural History of the Californias"
Series Editor—Lowell Lindsay

Southern California Series:

Geology Terms in English and Spanish	Aurand
Portrait of Paloma: A Novel	Crosby
Orange County: A Photographic Collection	Hemphill
California's El Camino Real and its Historic Bells	Kurillo
Mission Memoirs: Reflections on California's Past	Ruscin
Warbird Watcher's Guide to the Southern California Skies	Smith
Campgrounds of Santa Barbara and Ventura Counties	Tyler
Campgrounds of Los Angeles and Orange Counties	Tyler

California Desert Series:

Anza-Borrego A to Z: People, Places, and Things	D. Lindsay
The Anza-Borrego Desert Region (Wilderness Press)	L. and D. Lindsay
Geology of the Imperial/Mexicali Valleys (SDAG 1998)	L. Lindsay, ed.
Palm Springs Oasis: A Photographic Essay	Lawson
Desert Lore of Southern California, 2nd Ed.	Pepper
Peaks, Palms, and Picnics: Journeys in Coachella Valley	Pyle
Geology of Anza-Borrego: Edge of Creation	Remeika, Lindsay
Paleontology of Anza-Borrego (SDAG 1995)	Remeika, Sturz, eds.
California Desert Miracle: Parks and Wilderness	Wheat

Baja California Series:

The Other Side: Journeys in Baja California	Botello
Cave Paintings of Baja California, Rev. Ed.	Crosby
Backroad Baja: The Central Region	Higginbotham
Lost Cabos: The Way it Was (Lost Cabos Press)	Jackson
Journey with a Baja Burro	Mackintosh
Houses of Los Cabos (Amaroma)	Martinez, ed.
Mexicoland: Stories from Todos Santos (Barking Dog Books)	Mercer
Baja Legends: Historic Characters, Events, Locations	Niemann
Loreto, Baja California: First Capital (Tio Press)	O'Neil
Baja Outpost: The Guest Book from Patchen's Cabin	Patchen
Sea of Cortez Review	Redmond

San Diego Series:

Rise and Fall of San Diego: 150 Million Years	Abbott
Only in America	Alessio
More Adventures with Kids in San Diego	Botello, Paxton

Geology of San Diego: Journeys Through Time	Clifford, Bergen, Spear
Mission Trails Regional Park Trail Map	Cook
Cycling San Diego, 3rd Edition	Copp, Schad
A Good Camp: Gold Mines of Julian and the Cuyamacas	Fetzer
San Diego Mountain Bike Guide	Greenstadt
Geology of S.D. Metropolitan Area (CDMG Bulletin 200)	Kennedy, Peterson
San Diego Specters: Ghosts, Poltergeists, Tales	Lamb
Discover San Diego, 16th Ed.	Peik
San Diego: An Introduction to the Region (3rd Ed.)	Pryde
Campgrounds of San Diego County	Tyler
Peninsular Ranges: San Diego Back Country (Kendall/Hunt)	Walawender

Sunbelt Publications

Incorporated in 1988 with roots in publishing since 1973, Sunbelt produces and distributes publications about "Adventures in Natural and Cultural History." These include natural science and outdoor guidebooks, regional histories and reference books, multi-language pictorials, and stories that celebrate the land and its people.

Our publishing program focuses on the Californias which are today three states in two nations sharing one Pacific shore. Sunbelt books help to discover and conserve the natural and historical heritage of unique regions on the frontiers of adventure and learning. Our books guide readers into distinctive communities and special places, both natural and man-made.

**GENERAL GEOLOGIC MAP OF THE
JULIAN AND CUYAMACA MINING AREA,
SAN DIEGO COUNTY, CALIFORNIA**

`Qal,Ql,Qt`
(yellow) Alluvium-streambed and valley fill, flood plain, terraces.
`Kgr`
(light pink) Granitic rocks, undivided. Quartz diorite (tonalite).
`Kgb`
(dark pink) Cuyamaca Gabbro.
`hyb`
(green) Hybrid gneisses, granodiorite, quartz diorite.
`m`
(blue) Metasedimentary rocks. Julian Schist

Numbers refer to mines and minerals described in the source.
Explanation above is by Lowell Lindsay based on the source.
Map opposite is excerpted from Plate 1 in Weber 1963. *CDMG County Report 3.*
Compare to similar map in Fetzer 2002. *A Good Camp.* Chapter 1, Figure 1.